# Optimizing SQL

*Peter Gulutzan and Trudy Pelzer*

R&D Publications, Inc.
Lawrence, Kansas 66046

R&D Publications, Inc.
1601 West 23rd Street, Suite 200
Lawrence, Kansas 66046
USA

Trademarks:
dBase, dBase IV; Borland International, Inc.
dSalvage; Comtech Publishing, Ltd.
R+R; Concentric Data Systems, Inc.
Crystal; Crystal Computer Services, Inc.
DB2, OS/2, OS/2 Data Manager; International Business Machines Corp.
MS-DOS, Windows, Windows NT, FoxPro, Access, SMARTDRV; Microsoft Corp.
NEXTSTEP 486; NeXT Computers, Inc.
NetWare; Novell, Inc.
Ocelot; Ocelot Computer Services, Inc.
Oracle; Oracle Corp.
Q+E; Pioneer Software
Sybase; Sybase, Inc.
The Norton Utilities; Symantec Corp.
XDB; XDB Systems, Inc.
UNIX; X/Open Company, Ltd.

All trademarks (those above and any others mentioned in this book) are the property of their respective owners.

Distributed by **Prentice Hall**
**ISBN 0-13-100215-5**

*Cover Design: T. Watson Bogaard*

# Preface

## Why a Book on Optimizing SQL?

So what have we got that's new, or "oft was thought but ne'r so well expressed?" Too much of the writing on this subject is either in the "*SQL for Dummies*" vein — tedious restatements of a user's manual — or else in the purely academic catagory of "relational theory" — abstract tomes that play to the orthodoxy without the slightest attention to what programmers actually do and how they think. Our goal was to write a practical book for C programmers that would demonstrate how to use SQL in C. An introductory book on chess doesn't stop with the rules of moves, it show what happens in the games, and that's what we've tried to do here.

## Our Audience?

You don't need to be an SQL expert to understand this book, but we assume you know your C. In fact, we assume you're a working C programmer who is aware of the power of SQL and would like to learn to use it strategically in real applications. SQL programmers using any host language will benefit from our performance chapters (Chapters 7 and 8) which discuss optimizing SQL commands and the underlying structure of a database.

# What's in It?

Our emphasis is on the interface between SQL and C. Much of the book is devoted to the two main interface alternatives:

☐ embedded SQL

☐ ODBC

In each case we provide not only descriptions and explanations, but complete working programs as examples. Here's a bit of what's ahead:

☐ Chapter 2 is strictly SQL. Fluent English conversations happen with only 10 percent of English's vocabulary and zero reference texts; this chapter is the 10 percent you need for fluent SQL.

☐ Chapter 3 is on embedded static SQL. Putting SQL statements directly into a C "host program" is the conventional way to make database application programs, so the details are worth describing.

☐ Chapter 4 describes embedded dynamic SQL and finishes the topic of putting SQL directly into a C program. It includes a large example program that can serve as an on-line ad hoc query interface to an SQL database engine.

☐ Chapter 5 discusses the current hot topic, Microsoft's "Open Database Connectivity," or ODBC, application programming interface. We concentrate on a detailed description of the essential "core" calls. The descriptive text culminates in a complete ODBC application program that does something "real," namely, importing data from a *.DBF* file and putting it in an SQL database.

☐ Chapter 6 talks about indexes. Because the presence (or absence) of an index is often so crucial to performance, Chapter 6 includes a "toolkit" program (in both embedded SQL and ODBC) that determines whether an index exists for a given column.

☐ Chapter 7 is our "performance tips" chapter. This might seem like a tough topic for a book which isn't concentrating on a specific SQL package, but quite a few times we've found that how you choose to express an SQL command can affect performance, and when it does, it affects multiple packages the same way. We have all had minor eurekas like, "If I reverse these two expressions it takes 100 times longer" — stuff that shouldn't happen, so it isn't in a book written from another perspective. We will demonstrate with well-documented examples how, and why, you really can optimize the syntax of queries in SQL.

☐ In Chapter 8 we continue with some more performance issues. Unlike the tips in Chapter 7, where our main interest was choosing the best-performing SQL syntax, our main interest in Chapter 8 is the underlying structure of the database and how this structure affects storage and speed, sometimes unavoidably.

☐ In the Appendix we list the available SQL packages, along with whatever remarks about them we thought might be interesting, as well as some other information on SQL books, standards organizations, etc.

## *Why Read It?*

We are not professional authors or theorists. We're in the microcomputer programming business, and we've had some interesting experiences with SQL. Perhaps you envision a pair of ancient-mariner types grabbing wedding guests and quothing, "There was a ship!" But in fact, our idea of what's interesting really might correspond with yours, because in fact we might be a little bit like you.

# Table of Contents

# Chapter 1

# *Why a Book on SQL and C?*

In 640 A.D., the armies of Omar the Caliph swept out of Arabia and conquered Egypt. Omar observed that all books either agreed with the Koran — in which case they were superfluous — or they disagreed with the Koran — in which case they were impious. So he ordered that all the books in the Library of Alexandria be burned.

1354 years later, this possible-legendary pyromaniac potentate prompts us to introduce this book by saying that we have, we hope, not merely rehashed a subject which already has been covered, but at the same time we have tried to avoid making observations which would shock or disgust the orthodox practitioner of the database programming arts.

That the temptations exist in both directions, though, is evidence that this field is well trodden by humdrum texts of the "*Introduction to C*" or "*SQL for Dummies*" variety, and mines of controversy occasionally explode in the form of condemnations from people who want to preserve dogmas like "relational theory" or "correct programming style." It just goes to show that lots of people think this field is important and get excited by it. We do too. Our 15 years of combined experience in SQL and C have had almost no boring periods, and if you don't come away from this book with amazement at both SQL's power and its strangeness — well, then, the fault certainly isn't inherent in the subject matter.

Let's begin by talking about programming power. Figure 1.1 is a graph that appears to be proving an utterly ridiculous point. You may have seen this chart before; Sequiter Software, Inc. uses it in advertisements to imply that you'll get better performance with C and their library than you will with products like dBASE. But who would ever *want* to calculate the Sieve of Eratosthenes in a database language?

Let's give dBASE and its clones an equaller opportunity in a rematch. Suppose we base a benchmark on an episode in the writings of Eratosthenes's predecessor, the historian Herodotus: "Xerxes divided the Persian host into groups according to their national origins. He then had the men in each group counted, and found that the Persians constituted the largest group, followed by various other nationalities (Lydians, Bactrians, etc.), and that the Greeks were the smallest group." Figure 1.2 shows the time to *program* the Muster of Xerxes.

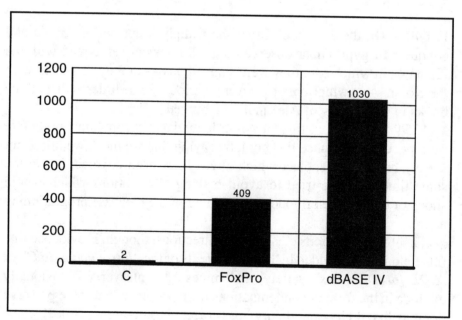

**Figure 1.1**    *Time to calculate the Sieve of Eratosthenes, in seconds.[1]*

It didn't take much time to program the Muster of Xerxes in the database languages because the latest versions of dBASE and FoxPro include some SQL capability. We could group the men, count the number in each group, and order by that count showing the largest group first using the following SQL statement:

```
SELECT NATION, COUNT(*) FROM HOST
    GROUP BY NATION ORDER BY 2 DESC;
```

We wrote a C program that does the same thing, but it's too large to include here. Briefly: we declared a string array for nations and a long-integer array for the count, then we opened a *.DBF* file and read every record in it (a *.DBF* file is a standard dBASE file). For each record, we searched the string array for a matching nation, adding a new array element if there was no match. Then we incremented the long-integer array for the equivalent index; that is, if "Paphlagonian" was the third string element then we *++d counter[3]*. After we'd finished reading, we bubble-sorted the long-integer array, making sure that when we interchanged elements of the long-integer array that we also interchanged the

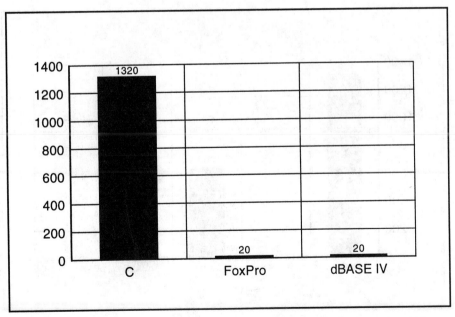

**Figure 1.2**    *Time to program the Muster of Xerxes, in seconds.*

corresponding elements in the string array. In all, including design time and debugging time, this took 1,320 seconds (22 minutes).

Of course, the fact that the design has some obvious flaws doesn't prove that we're stupider than normal programmers, who we assume couldn't do much better. The stupidity lies in doing the task at all. Who would ever *want* to code the Muster of Xerxes in a non-database language?

But Figure 1.2 is too kind to dBASE IV and FoxPro. They didn't win this race on the merits of their indexed-search-engine (ISE) capabilities — what we traditionally think of when we hear the terms "dBASE" or "xBASE." They won because Borland and Microsoft have injected a foreign substance into their products. It's the SQL steroid that won.

A fair race would pit the various generic language products, both with and without injections (see Figure 1.3). Since the two front runners are both using the same SQL *SELECT* statement, they have the same time as in Figure 1.2, and so does the trailer, unaided C. The guys in the middle are dBASE running on its own steam (all dBASE clones have an ISE) and C running with an add-on ISE library. The ISE programs get a little

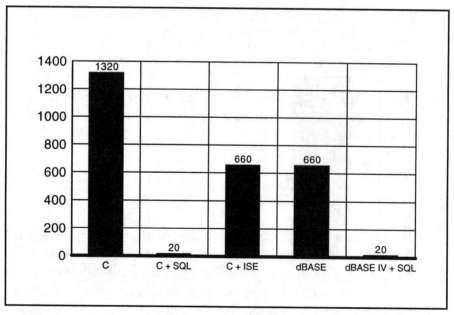

**Figure 1.3**    *Time to program the Muster of Xerxes, in seconds (revised).*

extra oomph because they have built-in "read record" capabilities, but they still have to process one record at a time like the C program does. Only with SQL can we work with groups, which is what big-picture administrators like Xerxes care about.

However, SQL can't run a race on its own, any more than a steroid can. It needs a host body, such as dBASE or C, to announce the results. (dBASE has a *SAY* statement and C has a *printf* function for this purpose, but SQL has no equivalent.) By design, SQL is a sub-language which is only useful for manipulating a database. C and dBASE are full languages, usable for all tasks, but as this example illustrates, they sometimes work better when they can call upon SQL.

Are there many questions in this Muster category? Yes, and we think the proof can be found by comparing the professional-programmer-coding-time-in-minutes to answer the following questions, all of which are quite different, but all of which can be translated to simple SQL queries:

"Who are the Athenians (in alphabetical order, without repeating names)?"

```
SELECT DISTINCT NAME FROM HOST WHERE NATION = 'ATHENS'
ORDER BY NAME;
```

"Is there a guy named Eratosthenes among the Greeks or the Lydians?"

```
SELECT NAME FROM HOST WHERE
NAME='ERATOSTHENES' AND NATION IN ('GREECE', 'LYDIA');
```

"I have a separate list showing nations and their Rebelliousness Quotient. How much of my army comes from nations whose RQ is greater than average?"

```
SELECT COUNT(*) FROM HOST WHERE NATION IN
    (SELECT NATION FROM NRQ WHERE RQ >
        (SELECT AVG(RQ) FROM NRQ));
```

Even the most complicated of these queries requires only 18 words to code. We invite you to finish the proof by writing equivalent programs in C and/or dBASE, or in any other language that doesn't have an SQL attachment. Since we know the number of words is only a rough indicator of complexity, we won't insist that the programs be 18 words or less. How about 500 or less? If you don't want to bother, you've just proved the point: programmers don't waste time doing it the hard way if somebody's already shown them the easy way.

Figure 1.3 establishes that SQL + (dBASE or C) is the winner in the "Muster" category, and Figure 1.1 shows that C is the clear winner in the "Sieve" category. Are we leading, then, to the conclusion that SQL + C is the overall winner?

We can't conclude that if the first race was unfair. Is it an accident that, for example, a *while* loop in the Borland C++ compiler is faster than a *while* loop in the Borland dBASE IV interpreter? In other words, if we used a future dBASE compiler, would we pull even?

It's theoretically possible, but it isn't likely anytime soon for a simple reason: specialization. People who work on database projects tend to be experts in databases (unlike people who work on language projects, who tend to be experts in languages). And what motive do database people have to become language experts when they know that what they're measured on is database capability? So no, it is not an accident that dBASE (or for that matter, any "database language") has merely a subset of the +s and *while*s and *if*s found in C, implemented in a measurably less efficient manner. The guys who write database programs don't care about Sieves.

Is a quick-executing Sieve as important as a quickly-coded Muster? Well, no, but don't get mixed up by old saws like "a programmer's time is far more expensive than a machine's time." That's not the issue here, because you can't code the Sieve in dBASE faster than in C. You have to use essentially the same syntax. The question is reduced, then, to this: "Is it worth it to make programs go faster if it costs nothing?"

We ran a profiler on a program in a report-writing package that we sell, a pretty archetypal SQL application, and found that 80 percent of the program's time was spent in the C code, doing screen input/output, calculating margins, counting lines, comparing break values with each other, storing variables, and handling all the other housekeeping tasks that happen in a typical application program. By no coincidence, benchmarks like the Sieve of Eratosthenes are designed to measure just that sort of "typical" stuff, so the benefits of C as a host are indeed significant to the overall performance.

Not only is C faster, it has more friends. A look in any software catalog will tell you that the number of add-ons for C far outnumber those for dBASE and its clones.

From this, we draw our conclusion: use C for Sieve parts of an application and SQL for Musters. All alternatives have been tested, tested again, weighed, and found wanting. SQL+C is not a matter of taste or opinion. It is a choice forced by fact.

## *Reference*

1. Source: Computer Associates International, Inc.

# Chapter 2

# *What SQL Statements Mean*

Like C, SQL has some basic rules for data conversions, delimiters, and the precedence of operators. As a C programmer, you have certain expectations about how a program will act given a specific set of instructions. It is easy to assume that the same type of instructions written in SQL will behave exactly the same way, but that isn't always the case. This chapter will examine the syntax of the major SQL commands in this book and contrast the effect of their execution with similar C commands where applicable. Note that, since this book is not intended as an SQL reference or tutorial, the syntax descriptions are necessarily brief — we have suppressed every option, every expressional nuance and every detail about SQL syntax that doesn't advance the plot. For those who want an equivalent to *SQL: The Complete Reference*, we list the organizations that are involved with SQL in the Appendix along with information on how to reach them.

## *BNF Notation*

We have used a common variant of the BNF notation for the syntax descriptions in this chapter:

☐ Words in capital letters are keywords and must be written exactly as shown (except that you have the choice of writing them in either upper- or lowercase letters).

☐ Words in lowercase letters represent syntactic categories. The words must be replaced with actual object names or constants.

☐ Square brackets [ and ] enclose optional items. The brackets are not part of the command and should not be typed.

☐ Single vertical bars | separate alternatives. Choose only one of the options listed. The vertical bars are not part of the command and should not be typed. (Caution: as we will see later, double vertical bars, ||, are SQL's concatenation operator.)

☐ Braces { and } indicate that the material enclosed in them consists of a set of several items (separated by vertical bars) from which exactly one is to be chosen. The braces are not part of the command and should not be typed.

☐ Ellipses ... mean the preceding term may be repeated one or more times. The ellipses are not part of the command and should not be typed.

☐ Where parentheses ( ) appear, they are part of the command and must be typed.

☐ SQL statements within a C program must end with a semicolon ;, and we'll terminate all of the examples in the book this way to avoid confusion.

In the simplified example:

```
CREATE TABLE table_name (column_name {INTEGER | CHAR(5)});
```

the words *CREATE, TABLE, INTEGER* and *CHAR* are SQL keywords and must be written without changes, as must the parentheses and the terminating semicolon. The words *table_name* and *column_name* must be replaced with names that follow SQL's rules for identifier names. The data type of the column can be either *INTEGER* or *CHAR(5)*. Based on this example, either of the following SQL statements is legal:

```
CREATE TABLE table1 (column1 INTEGER);
CREATE TABLE any_legal_name (any_legal_name CHAR(5));
```

# The SQL Standard

The American National Standards Institute (ANSI) X3H2 Database Standards Committee issued the first ANSI SQL standard in October, 1986. (We'll call this document SQL 86 throughout the book.) The first revision to the standard was released in 1989 (SQL 89), and the most recent revision in 1992 (SQL 92). SQL 92 includes the syntax of both SQL 86 and SQL 89 (with minor exceptions), plus new syntax to standardize many features that SQL DBMS vendors had already implemented prior to the 1992 standard. In this book, we'll concern ourselves mostly with entry level SQL 92 syntax.

# Commands and Syntax

SQL commands fall into three major catagories:

☐ Data Definition Language (DDL) consists of commands used to create, alter, and drop database objects, as well as to impose integrity constraints on tables.

☐ Data Manipulation Language (DML) consists of commands used to retrieve and change data. The four DML commands are the ones that application programs use the most.

☐ Data Control Language (DCL) consists of commands used to control security and access to data.

(There is an additional catagory of SQL commands that are used when embedding SQL in a host language. We will discuss these commands in Chapters 3 and 4.)

# *Expressions, Functions and Conditions*

In this book, we'll define *expressions* in an SQL statement to mean column names, constants, functions, or combinations of these items mixed with operators.

In SQL numeric expressions, constant values look like *5* or *5.5* or *-57.7*. The common arithmetic operators + – / and * are all supported, and (no surprise to C programmers) / and * have precedence over + and –, so for example, the expression *1 + 1 - 1 / 2* equals *1.5*.

In SQL string expressions, constant values look like *'X'* or *'The rain in Spain'* — that is, SQL constant strings are enclosed in single quotes, as in Pascal. Under no circumstances should constants be enclosed in double quotes, as in C. Of course, arithmetic operators can't be used on strings, but SQL does provide a special operator, ‖, which concatenates strings (no surprise to BASIC programmers although C has no precise equivalent), so for example, the expression *'a' ‖ 'b'* equals *'ab'*.

SQL *functions* are built into the language and are not user-definable as C functions are. We'll discuss functions in more detail when we look at the *select* statement.

*Conditions* are pairs of expressions which return a truth value. For example, in the C statement:

```
if (a < b) printf("a is less than b\n");
```

*a < b* is the condition, and the possible truth values are *0 (FALSE)* or *1 (TRUE)*.

There is no *if* statement in SQL because SQL, unlike C (which must give step-by-step instructions for every task), is non-procedural. But five of the SQL statements we describe herein can contain conditions.

The general form of an SQL comparison condition is:

```
<column_name | constant> <operator> <column_name | constant>
```

where *operator* is one of the comparison operators: equals =, not equals <>, less than <, less than or equal to <=, greater than >, and greater than or equal to >=.

Conditions can also be built with the SQL operators *BETWEEN, IN, LIKE, IS NULL*, or *EXISTS*, and, as with C, conditions can be combined with

Boolean operators (*AND, OR, NOT*) and with parentheses for greater complexity.

Here are some examples of simple SQL conditions, illustrating the major operators and the two main constant types (string and numeric):

```
numeric_column < 0                character_column < 'foo'
numeric_column = 0                character_column = 'foo'
numeric_column <> 0               character_column <> 'foo'
numeric_column >= 0               character_column >= 'foo'
numeric_column BETWEEN 0 and 1    character_column BETWEEN 'fon' AND 'foo'
numeric_column = 0 OR             character_column = 'fon' OR
    numeric_column = 1                character_column = 'foo'
numeric_column <> 0 AND           character_column <> 'fon' AND
    numeric_column <> 1               character_column <> 'foo'
numeric_column IN (1,5)           character_column IN ('foo', 'goo')
numeric_column NOT IN (1,5)       character_column NOT IN ('foo', 'goo')
numeric_column IS NULL            character_column IS NULL
                                  character_column LIKE 'foo%'
                                  character_column NOT LIKE 'foo%'
```

This listing shows another major difference between SQL and C. The comparison and Boolean operators in SQL are not quite the same as those in C. Although $<$, $<=$, $>$, and $>=$ mean the same thing, the SQL operator for equality is $=$ — not $==$ as in C. And the SQL operator for inequality is $<>$ — not $!=$ as in C. Additionally, SQL uses *AND* instead of C's &&, *OR* instead of C's ||, and *NOT* instead of C's !.

SQL's other operators can also be used to set fairly explicit conditions.

*BETWEEN* is used to find numeric or character data within a range of values. Its converse is *NOT BETWEEN*. The SQL condition *BETWEEN 0 AND 1* is equivalent to the C condition *(value>=0 && value<=1)*. Note that we shouldn't take the English meaning of "between" too seriously. The condition:

```
-2 BETWEEN -1 AND -3
```

is *FALSE*, because the expression is always, in effect, translated to the C equivalent:

```
(-2 >= -1 && -2 <= -3)
```

which is not the ordinary English meaning of "between."

*IN* is used to find numeric or character data which matches one of a specified set of values. Its converse is *NOT IN*. The SQL condition *IN (1,5)* is equivalent to the C condition *(value==1 || value ==5)*; that is:

```
a IN (x, y)
```

is merely shorthand for:

```
a = x OR a = y
```

*IS NULL* is used to test numeric or character fields for the presence of *NULL*s. Its converse is *IS NOT NULL*. *NULL*s are a major difference between SQL and C. Many C programs and include files start with *#define NULL 0* or *#define NULL 0L*, but in SQL, a *NULL* is not a zero or a null-terminated string. It is a marker used to represent missing information, with no equivalent in C. Although a *NULL* is not really a value, you can think of it as an unknown value, or an inapplicable value, or an absence of value. Thus, unlike C, SQL has three possible truth values because comparisons with SQL's *NULL*s (which don't exist in C) yield neither *TRUE* nor *FALSE* — they yield *UNKNOWN*. The *UNKNOWN* truth value can be interpreted as "maybe," "who cares?," or "don't know," but whatever the interpretation, the following statement is perfectly good C logic, yet dubious SQL logic:

If the expression *x<y* is *FALSE*, then the expression *x>=y* must be *TRUE*.

A mistake is possible if there is a chance that either *x* or *y* is *NULL*.

*LIKE* is used to find character data that matches a specified pattern. Its converse is *NOT LIKE*. The SQL condition *column_name LIKE 'foo%'* is equivalent to the C condition *strncmpi(column_name, "foo", 3)*. The percent sign in a *LIKE* pattern is a wildcard signal meaning "any character or characters can be here." There is one other wildcard signal, the underline character, meaning "any character (but not more than one character) can be here." You can put any number of *%*s or _characters in the pattern string, in any position. Thus, the condition *LIKE 'F_F%'* means "a string of any length whose first and third characters must be *F*." Such conditions have no equivalent in C's standard library.

*EXISTS* takes the result of a subquery as an argument — if the subquery produces any rows at all, *EXISTS* returns *TRUE*; otherwise it returns *FALSE*. We'll discuss subqueries when we look at the *SELECT* statement.

## Data Types

The major SQL data types are *SMALLINT, INTEGER, DECIMAL, FLOAT, DOUBLE, DATE, TIME, TIMESTAMP, CHAR*, and *VARCHAR*.

The precision of the *SMALLINT* and *INTEGER* data types is another major difference between SQL and C. The *INTEGER* data type does not mean "a whole number between –32767 and +32767" because in SQL the *INTEGER* type has a range between –2,147,483,648 and +2,147,483,647 (perhaps not a surprise when you consider that SQL is common on 32-bit machines). So the 16-bit-C equivalent is not *int*, it is *long int*. The SQL data type for 16-bit integers is *SMALLINT*.

The *DECIMAL* data type is used for fixed-point numbers (as opposed to floating-point numbers which are *FLOAT* or *DOUBLE*).

*CHAR* is similar to C's *char* type, but SQL's *CHAR* is for fixed-size strings. There is a variant data type, *VARCHAR*, for varying-size strings. Although *CHAR* and *VARCHAR* equate with C's *char* type, you'll need to define them with different sizes because when you have an SQL column with 5 characters, e.g.:

```
CREATE TABLE table2 (column2 CHAR(5));
```

you can store the value *'abcde'* in it. To store *"abcde"* in a C string, you'd need to define it as *char c[6]* because, of course, C strings end with \0.

When you assign a data type to an SQL column, are you telling the DBMS how the data should be stored? No. The designers of the DBMS decide how to store data, and you as an application programmer can only give hints. We'll get to the storage details in Chapter 8; for now, it's best just to know that SQL data types describe ranges and sizes, but the physical details are not your concern — a theme which repeats, as you will see.

# *Data Definition Language (DDL)*

We'll start our discussion of SQL commands with SQL DDL because you can't do anything with an object until you've created it. The DDL commands we'll look at are CREATE TABLE, DROP TABLE, CREATE INDEX, DROP INDEX, CREATE VIEW, and DROP VIEW.

## *CREATE TABLE*

```
Syntax: CREATE TABLE table_name
        (column_name data-type [NOT NULL] [, ...]
        [, PRIMARY KEY (column_name [, ...])]
        [, FOREIGN KEY (column_name) REFERENCES table_name [, ...]])
        [CHECK (condition)];
```

CREATE TABLE creates a table and defines its structure. Here's the simplest example possible:

```
CREATE TABLE table1 (column1 INTEGER);
```

This command creates a table named *table1* and specifies that it will have one column (called *column1*) which will hold an integer value in each record inserted into the table. A table can be thought of as a bunch of structured data. Think of C's *struct {...} table1;*, that is, a definition of a structure which is accompanied by precisely one instance of the structure, and you won't be far off.

Here are some other examples of CREATE TABLE statements with a variety of columns, data types, and sizes:

```
CREATE TABLE figures
    (s1 INTEGER, s2 SMALLINT, s3 FLOAT, s4 DOUBLE);

CREATE TABLE moments (s1 DATE, s2 TIME);

CREATE TABLE dramatis_personae (name CHAR(20));
```

After the definition of the column's data type comes *[NOT NULL]*. That is, optionally we can express a constraint rule for the column thus:

```
CREATE TABLE dramatis_personae (name CHAR(20) NOT NULL);
```

The *name* records in this table may not have *NULL* as a value. Remember that you can think of a *NULL* as an unknown value, or an inapplicable value, or an absence of value. Why would we use *NULLs*?

Question: "How many daughters did Macbeth have?" Answer: zero.

Question: "What was the name of Macbeth's daughter?" Answer: *NULL*, because Macbeth had no daughters. Notice that this is very different from the answer: <blank space>, which would imply that Macbeth had a daughter with no name.

Question: "What's he that's not of woman born?" Answer: *NULL*, because it's a riddle, but at the end of the play we find out the answer is "Macduff", so the *NULL* was just a placeholder. There *was* a value; we just didn't know what it was.

Two more questions: "How many daughters did I-forget-his-name have?" and "What was the name of whozits's daughter?" Answers: Don't be silly. If we can't identify the person, we can't answer anything about him/her. That is: if we're making a table to answer that kind of question, we must constrain the *name* field to *NOT NULL* values, because there's no point in allowing data entries where such an essential item is allowed to be missing or unknown.

A column that uniquely identifies a record can be designated the primary key of a table. The primary key is defined as follows:

```
[, PRIMARY KEY (column_name)]
```

In the record:

```
name:         Macbeth
description:  Scots Male
occupation:   Thane of Glamis
              Thane of Cawdor
              King of Scotland
```

only the *name* column is a candidate for the table's primary key. We can't use *Description* because it doesn't uniquely identify one person — if we asked, "How many daughters did the Scots Male have?" we'd get an unpredictable answer because other Scots males (Macduff, for instance) may be in the database too.

*Occupation* is no good either. This guy kept picking up new jobs, so the question, "How many daughters did the Thane of Glamis have?" is only going to sum his offspring after he became Thane of Glamis; that's transient information.

For this record, we'd make the following table:

```
CREATE TABLE dramatis_personae
    (name CHAR(20) NOT NULL, description CHAR(25),
    occupation1 VARCHAR(50), occupation_2 VARCHAR(50),
    occupation3 VARCHAR(50), PRIMARY KEY (name));
```

The *dramatis_personae* table provides the name, description, and occupation data, with *name* as the primary key. Envision a part of the database:

| name | description | occupation1 | occupation2 | occupation3 |
|------|-------------|-------------|-------------|-------------|
| Macbeth | Scots Male | Thane of Glamis | Thane of Cawdor | King of Scotland |
| Macduff | Scots Male | Thane of Fife | NULL | NULL |

You'll notice that Macbeth fits our structure perfectly, but we've revealed a bit of information about Macduff that we didn't anticipate when we designed the table. Macduff was always and only the Thane of Fife, not a moonlighter like Macbeth, so we had to fill in *occupation2* and *occupation3* with *NULL* ("not applicable"), meaning "Macduff didn't have a second or a third job."

But — a flaw in SQL that has generated some controversy — *NULL* can stand for "unknown" just as easily as for "not applicable", so the meaning might be "we don't know what Macduff's second occupation was." With the above structure, an SQL DBMS would have to answer the question "Was Macduff the Queen of England?" with "Don't know," and "How many occupations did Macduff have?" with "3." We can avoid incorrect or confusing answers like this by splitting the information into two separate tables and placing the name information in both of them as a link:

```
CREATE TABLE dramatis_personae
    (name CHAR(20) NOT NULL, description CHAR(25),
    PRIMARY KEY (name));
```

```
CREATE TABLE occupations
    (name CHAR(20) NOT NULL, occupation VARCHAR(50),
    FOREIGN KEY (name) REFERENCES dramatis_personae);
```

The data is now organized as:

| dramatis_personae | |
|---|---|
| **name** | **description** |
| Macbeth | Scots Male |
| Macduff | Scots Male |

| occupations | |
|---|---|
| **name** | **occupation** |
| Macbeth | Thane of Glamis |
| Macbeth | Thane of Cawdor |
| Macbeth | King of Scotland |
| Macduff | Thane of Fife |

This is a better organization because we have eliminated the ambiguous *NULL*s, yet no information is lost. As long as the *occupations* table contains a copy of the *dramatis_personae* table's primary key, the *name* column can be used to join these tables. The *name* copy in *occupations* is called the foreign key, and it is said to reference the *dramatis_personae* table, because it cannot contain any values (except *NULL*) that *dramatis_personae* doesn't contain in its *name* column. Therefore, we have to ensure that we can't put anybody into *occupations* who isn't in *dramatis_personae* and that we can't delete anybody from *dramatis_personae* if there's a record for him/her in *occupations*. Either of those cases would result in the equivalent of a "dangling pointer" in C. Such a situation is called a violation of referential integrity. The optional clause:

```
[, FOREIGN KEY (column_name) REFERENCES table_name]
```

declares that a column in a table is a foreign key referencing another table and tells the DBMS that it is responsible for maintaining referential integrity.

SQL 92 provides an *ON DELETE* clause for the foreign key definition, which tells the DBMS what to do when a user tries to delete a primary key that would leave a dangling foreign key. The options are *SET NULL*, *SET DEFAULT*, *NO ACTION* (some DBMSs use *RESTRICT* instead), and *CASCADE*. *SET NULL* sets the foreign key to *NULL*, and *SET DEFAULT* sets it to its default value, before deleting the primary key. *RESTRICT* disallows the deletion. *CASCADE* tells the DBMS it's okay to delete the primary key as long as it also deletes all foreign keys with the same value.

The *CHECK* clause:

```
[CHECK (condition)]
```

prevents the insertion of records that don't match the specified condition.

Suppose we held the common belief that names beginning with "Mac" are Scottish, while names beginning with "Mc" are Irish. Knowing that there are no Irishmen in Macbeth, we decide to guard against spelling mistakes by specifying that names must not begin with "Mc." This is done with the condition:

```
name NOT LIKE 'Mc%'
```

(Since the *name* column is defined as *NOT NULL*, the "three-value truth table" pitfall described on page 14 doesn't apply to this condition.)

With this spell checker installed, with some format changes (spacing doesn't matter in SQL any more than it does in C), and keeping the referential integrity rules, the definition of the two tables now looks like this:

```
CREATE TABLE dramatis_personae
    (name CHAR(20) NOT NULL, description CHAR(25),
    PRIMARY KEY (name)) CHECK (name NOT LIKE 'Mc%');

CREATE TABLE occupations
    (name CHAR(20) NOT NULL, occupation VARCHAR(50),
    FOREIGN KEY (name) REFERENCES dramatis_personae);
```

## DROP TABLE

Syntax: DROP TABLE table_name;

When we want to get rid of something that we created we *DROP* it. The statement:

```
DROP TABLE table1;
```

removes the contents *and* the structure definition of *table1* from the database. This is in contrast with the DML *DELETE* statement, which only gets rid of the contents of the table.

*DELETE* empties the box, while *DROP* empties the box and throws the box away.

### CREATE INDEX

```
Syntax: CREATE [UNIQUE] INDEX index_name
        ON table_name (column_name [{ASC | DESC}] [, ...]);
```

You will not find any mention of indexes in the ANSI SQL standard, but every serious SQL product supports *CREATE INDEX*, so we acknowledge that this command is part of the *de facto* SQL standard. Its effect is that the DBMS creates a B-tree index on the column(s) you specify, with the keys sorted in either ascending *(ASC)* or descending *(DESC)* order. If you use the optional keyword *UNIQUE*, the DBMS will also ensure that duplicate values are not permitted in the index key.

Creating an index can reduce search time. See Chapter 6 for more on indexes.

### DROP INDEX

```
Syntax: DROP INDEX index_name;
```

This command is analogous to *DROP TABLE* because the effect is that the index is destroyed — all the index keys are deleted, and the definition of the index is destroyed as well.

### CREATE VIEW

```
Syntax: CREATE VIEW view_name AS select_statement WITH CHECK OPTION;
```

Tables that we make with *CREATE TABLE* are called base tables. Tables that we make with *CREATE VIEW* are called views or virtual tables. A base table has some tenuous hold on physical reality which a view table lacks, but in most DML statements you can use base tables or views interchangeably.

The *select_statement* defines the view. We won't describe *SELECT* until we talk about DML, but basically, at any time, a view consists of the rows that would result if the *select_statement* were executed.

The optional *WITH CHECK OPTION* clause ensures that any update operations (that is, any *INSERT*, *UPDATE*, or *DELETE*) performed on the view will be checked to see if the change conforms to the view's definition. A change that does not conform will be rejected. Without this clause, non-conforming changes will still be accepted by the base table(s) that underlies the view.

An example:

```
CREATE VIEW view_jobs AS SELECT * FROM occupations;
```

creates a view called *view_jobs*, which is an exact copy of the *occupations* table.

### DROP VIEW

```
Syntax: DROP VIEW view_name;
```

Perhaps inconsistently, the reverse of *CREATE VIEW*, which is *DROP VIEW*, doesn't work in the same way that *DROP TABLE* does. Unlike *DROP TABLE* , which actually removes data from the database before removing the table's definition, the statement:

```
DROP VIEW view_jobs;
```

removes only the view definition — there is no effect on data.

## Data Manipulation Language (DML)

The DML commands *INSERT*, *SELECT*, *UPDATE*, and *DELETE* are the most common SQL statements in a database application.

### INSERT

```
Syntax: INSERT INTO table_name
        VALUES (constant [, ...] | NULL);
```

*INSERT* puts data into a table the way that C's *strcpy* puts values into a structure's components, except that *INSERT* fills one entire table row, or record, in a single execution using the constants provided in the *VALUES* clause. If the constants are strings, enclose them in single quote marks; if they're numbers, leave off the quote marks. Either way, separate the constants in the *VALUES* clause with commas.

Here are some *INSERT* statements we could use to fill the Macbeth tables:

```
INSERT INTO dramatis_personae VALUES ('Macbeth','Scots Male');
INSERT INTO dramatis_personae VALUES ('Macduff','Scots Male');
INSERT INTO occupations VALUES ('Macbeth','Thane of Glamis');
INSERT INTO occupations VALUES ('Macbeth','Thane of Cawdor');
INSERT INTO occupations VALUES ('Macbeth','King of Scotland');
INSERT INTO occupations VALUES ('Macduff','Thane of Fife');
```

Due to the constraints set when a table is created, an *INSERT* will fail under the following conditions:

☐ attempts to insert data which isn't the same type as a column's data type;

☐ attempts to insert *NULLs* into a *NOT NULL* column;

☐ attempts to insert duplicates into a *UNIQUE* or *PRIMARY* key;

☐ attempts to insert data into a *FOREIGN KEY* when that value doesn't already exist in the referenced *PRIMARY KEY*;

☐ attempts to insert data which doesn't conform to a *CHECK* condition.

Thus, the statement:

```
INSERT INTO dramatis_personae VALUES ('Macduff','Motherless Child');
```

would be rejected by the DBMS because there's already a row in the table with *name='Macduff'*; *name* is the primary key and primary keys are unique, that is, you can't have more than one with the same value.

## SELECT

```
Syntax: SELECT [DISTINCT] {* | column_name | expression [, ...]}
        FROM table_name [, ...]
        [WHERE condition]
        [GROUP BY column_name [, ...] [HAVING condition]]
        UNION [ALL] select_statement
        [ORDER BY {column_name | column_number} [{ASC | DESC}] [, ...]];
```

The *SELECT* statement obtains data from the database. The command:

```
SELECT name FROM occupations;
```

finds all the records in the *occupations* table, but returns only the *name* column for each record found, a process known as projection. The result is:

| name |
|------|
| Macbeth |
| Macbeth |
| Macbeth |
| Macduff |

```
SELECT DISTINCT name FROM occupations;
```

also finds all the records in the *occupations* table, returning only the *name* column for each. But the specification *DISTINCT* then causes the SQL engine to eliminate duplicate records, so we don't see Macbeth repeated. The result is:

| name |
|------|
| Macbeth |
| Macduff |

The commands:

```
SELECT name, description FROM dramatis_personae;
SELECT * FROM dramatis_personae;
```

find all the records in *dramatis_personae* and return both the *name* and the *description* column values. The asterisk, *, is shorthand for "all columns." The result is:

| name | description |
|---|---|
| Macbeth | Scots Male |
| Macduff | Scots Male |

The *WHERE* clause in a DML statement specifies the condition that must be met for data to be included in the result. For example:

```
SELECT * FROM dramatis_personae WHERE name = 'Macbeth';
```

finds all the records in the *dramatis_personae* table which match the condition, that is, where the contents of the *name* column = *Macbeth*. This process is known as filtering.

The command:

```
SELECT * FROM dramatis_personae, occupations;
```

is a join. We are selecting from two tables at once, and we want all the data in both the *dramatis_personae* and the *occupations* tables. If you look at the result, you will see that every record of the *dramatis_personae* table has been matched with every record of the *occupations* table, even if the records have nothing to do with each other:

| name | description | name | occupation |
|---|---|---|---|
| Macbeth | Scots Male | Macbeth | Thane of Glamis |
| Macbeth | Scots Male | Macbeth | Thane of Cawdor |
| Macbeth | Scots Male | Macbeth | King of Scotland |
| Macbeth | Scots Male | Macduff | Thane of Fife |
| Macduff | Scots Male | Macbeth | Thane of Glamis |
| Macduff | Scots Male | Macbeth | Thane of Cawdor |
| Macduff | Scots Male | Macbeth | King of Scotland |
| Macduff | Scots Male | Macduff | Thane of Fife |

This type of join is a Cartesian join. A Cartesian join makes logical sense but normally has no use in the real world. In this join, for instance, the DBMS was forced to expend computer resources pairing Macduff's description with Macbeth's occupations (and Macbeth's description with Macduff's occupation). The *WHERE* clause can be used to apply a constraint to the join, so that only matching records are combined, as follows:

```
SELECT * FROM dramatis_personae, occupations
    WHERE dramatis_personae.name = occupations.name;
```

When we join using a matching "=" expression, the result is an equijoin. We are again selecting from two tables at once, but this time we insist that the *name* column in the *dramatis_personae* table must match the *name* column in the *occupations* table. Notice how the qualified form <table_name>.<column_name> has to be used in the *WHERE* clause because <column_name> alone would be ambiguous; the construct, *dramatis_personae.name*, can be compared with C's *structure_name.component_name*, where a period is similarly used. The result of the equijoin is:

| name | description | name | occupation |
|---|---|---|---|
| Macbeth | Scots Male | Macbeth | Thane of Glamis |
| Macbeth | Scots Male | Macbeth | Thane of Cawdor |
| Macbeth | Scots Male | Macbeth | King of Scotland |
| Macduff | Scots Male | Macduff | Thane of Fife |

The *GROUP BY* clause is used for aggregation:

```
SELECT name FROM occupations GROUP BY name;
```

This is a simple aggregation command. We take all of the *Macbeths* in the *occupations* table and put them in one pigeonhole. Then we take all of the *Macduff*s in the *occupations* table and put them in another pigeonhole. Finally, we show the two pigeonholes:

| name |
|------|
| Macbeth |
| Macduff |

The result in this simple example looks no different from the result we got with *SELECT DISTINCT name FROM occupations;*, and in fact it is better to use *SELECT DISTINCT...* rather than *SELECT... GROUP BY...* if all you want to see is grouped columns. But we can do more with *GROUP BY*:

```
SELECT name, COUNT(name) FROM occupations GROUP BY name;
```

This is an aggregation with an aggregate function, namely the built-in SQL function *COUNT(column_name)*. With this function you get a tally of the number of times each of the (non-*NULL*) grouped column names occurred. Since Macbeth had three occupations while Macduff had only one, the result is:

| name | count |
|------|-------|
| Macbeth | 3 |
| Macduff | 1 |

There are four other aggregate functions, all of which also operate on the non-*NULL* values in their argument: *MIN(column_name)* for minimums, *MAX(column_name)* for maximums, *AVG(column_name)* for averages of numeric columns, and *SUM(column_name)* for totals of numeric columns.

Because they operate on non-*NULL* values, aggregate functions can return some unexpected results. For example, suppose we have a two-column table, as shown in the following diagram:

| column_a | column_b |
|----------|----------|
| 1        | 1        |
| NULL     | 1        |

The query:

```
SELECT SUM(column_a) + SUM(column_b) FROM table;
```

would return *3* (proof: *SUM* eliminates *NULLs*, so *SUM(column_a)=1* and *SUM(column_b)=2* and *1+2=3*).

However, the following query, which at first appears to be totally equivalent:

```
SELECT SUM(column_a+column_b) FROM table;
```

would return *2* (proof: for record *1*, *1+1=2* and for record *2*, *NULL+1=NULL* because all operations on *NULL* return *NULL*, so *SUM*, which eliminates *NULLs* before summing, comes up with a total of *2*). The same problem can occur with the other aggregate functions.

There is also a variant of *COUNT(column_name)*, namely *COUNT(\*)*, which doesn't eliminate *NULLs* beforehand:

```
SELECT name, COUNT(*) FROM occupations
    GROUP BY name HAVING COUNT(*) > 1;
```

The *HAVING* clause is like the *WHERE* clause in that it contains a condition, but this is an aggregation with a condition on the aggregation itself. A *HAVING* clause allows the DBMS to filter using an aggregate function. Since Macbeth has more than one occupation but Macduff doesn't, this command would return only the first of the two records the *GROUP BY* example returned:

| name | count |
|------|-------|
| Macbeth | 3 |

The *UNION* operator merges two results. For example:

```
SELECT name, occupation FROM occupations
    WHERE occupation like 'Thane%'
UNION
SELECT name, occupation FROM occupations
    WHERE occupation like 'King%';
```

A union of two sets is that set of values that appears in either set, but without duplication — that is, *UNION* returns distinct records from a set of two or more queries. To envision what *UNION* is doing, imagine that the two *SELECT*s in our example are run separately. The result of the first *SELECT* is:

| name | occupation |
|------|------------|
| Macbeth | Thane of Glamis |
| Macbeth | Thane of Cawdor |
| Macduff | Thane of Fife |

And the result of the second *SELECT* is:

| name | occupation |
|------|------------|
| Macbeth | King of Scotland |

Now simply paste one result after the other one. The combined result looks like this:

| name | occupation |
|------|------------|
| Macbeth | Thane of Glamis |
| Macbeth | Thane of Cawdor |
| Macduff | Thane of Fife |
| Macbeth | King of Scotland |

In this particular case, the same effect occurs with:

```
SELECT name, occupation FROM occupations
    WHERE occupation LIKE 'Thane%' OR occupation LIKE 'King%';
```

However, you have to use *UNION* when you're merging the results from two different queries on different tables.

The *ORDER BY* clause specifies the order in which the records are to be returned. The following two commands are equivalent:

```
SELECT name, occupation FROM occupations ORDER BY occupation ASC;
```

```
SELECT name, occupation FROM occupations ORDER BY 2;
```

The results come out in the ascending *(ASC)* alphabetical order of the *occupations* column. The other option is descending *(DESC)* order. (*ASC* is the default.) The variant *ORDER BY 2*, that is, "order by the second column in the *SELECT*," is deprecated by SQL 92.

Another difference between SQL and C is that when you call *quicksort()* from C, you know the routine will do a sort. The sort might go faster when the records are already in order, but the sort procedure will happen regardless. An SQL DBMS doesn't necessarily have to do a sort when it sees *ORDER BY column_name* — if the records in question are already in order (maybe they've been retrieved via an index), the SQL engine might do nothing at all. This shows a subtle difference between the C's and SQL's operating philosophies: C expresses *what* to do, SQL merely expresses what *result* is desired. In other words: C is procedural, while SQL is non-procedural, or descriptive.

SQL can use the output from one *SELECT* as the input for another *SELECT*. An illustration:

```
SELECT name FROM dramatis_personae WHERE name IN
    (SELECT name FROM occupations);
```

A rough description of what happens here is that the SQL engine must first process the inner *SELECT* or subquery — *SELECT name FROM occupations* — to get the result set: *name = 'Macbeth'*, *name = 'Macduff'* (we've omitted the duplicates). Then it plugs the result set into the outer *SELECT*, so that, effectively, the command now reads:

```
SELECT name FROM dramatis_personae
    WHERE name IN ('Macbeth', 'Macduff');
```

And this is the query whose result is returned.

Another subquery operator is *EXISTS*. For example:

```
SELECT name FROM dramatis_personae d WHERE EXISTS
    (SELECT * FROM occupations o WHERE o.name = d.name);
```

In this example an inner *SELECT* with a *WHERE* clause refers to a column in a table of the outer *SELECT*. This is known as a correlated subquery. (The "*d*" after *dramatis_personae* is an alias; later in the command we refer to "*d.name*," i.e., "the *name* column in table *d*, which is the *dramatis_personae* table in the outer *SELECT*".)

For our earlier, uncorrelated subquery using *IN*, the SQL engine was able to resolve the inner query first and pass the results to the outer query. A correlated subquery can't be handled so easily because the SQL engine has to find something in the outer query before it can do the inner one. But once it has done so, this *EXISTS* example will deliver the same result as the *IN* example; that is:

| name |
|------|
| Macbeth |
| Macduff |

## UPDATE

```
Syntax: UPDATE table_name SET column_name = constant | NULL [, ...]
    [WHERE condition];
```

*UPDATE* changes data in the columns named to the new values assigned by the *SET* clause. Like *INSERT*, *UPDATE* has built-in constraint checking and will fail if the new data doesn't conform to the constraints set during *CREATE TABLE*. Thus, the statement:

```
UPDATE occupations SET name = NULL;
```

would be rejected by the DBMS, which would return a message saying (approximately), "*name* is defined as *NOT NULL*, so you can't set it to *NULL*."

We've said before that C is a procedural language while SQL is a non-procedural, or descriptive, language. This subtle difference matters because a descriptive statement has no sense of time. Assignments in SQL do not happen in sequence as they do in C.

We can illustrate this with the following example. Given that *name = 'Macbeth'* and *description = 'Scots Male'*,

```
UPDATE dramatis_personae SET description = name, name = description;
```

would result in a transposition, that is: *name = 'Scots Male'* and *description = 'Macbeth'*. But a C program with the instructions:

```
strcpy(description,name); strcpy(name,description);
```

would come up with: *name = 'Macbeth'* and *description = 'Macbeth'*.

Every record in our *dramatis_personae* table contains a column named *description* that contains the value *Scots Male*. But these days the preferred term is "Scottish." Let's change our two-person database to reflect that:

```
UPDATE dramatis_personae SET description = 'Scottish Male';
```

And now, this late-breaking news: In the last scene of the play, the new king, Malcolm, upgrades all his thanes to earls. That applies to Macduff only (Macbeth dies in the second-last scene), so we must use *UPDATE* with a condition:

```
UPDATE occupations SET occupation = 'Earl of Fife'
    WHERE name = 'Macduff';
```

Notice that in the *UPDATE* statement's *SET* clause, = is an assignment operator (as it is in C), but in the *WHERE* clause = represents comparison (that is, it's comparable to C's == operator). There is no potential for ambiguity because the two types of equals operators cannot be mixed in the same clause.

## *DELETE*

```
Syntax: DELETE FROM table_name
        [WHERE condition];
```

*DELETE* erases all records of the table which satisfy the *WHERE* clause's condition. Come to think of it, since Macbeth is dead, he should be removed entirely from the database:

```
DELETE FROM occupations WHERE name = 'Macbeth';
DELETE FROM dramatis_personae WHERE name = 'Macbeth';
```

We have to delete all records about "Macbeth" from *occupations* first, because of the foreign key/primary key relationship between the two tables. If we try to delete from *dramatis_personae* first, the DBMS will reject the statement with the error message, "The *occupations* table has a foreign key *Macbeth* which references the row you're trying to delete, so deletion would be a referential-integrity violation."

If, however, the *CREATE TABLE* command had specified an *ON DELETE* clause:

```
CREATE TABLE occupations
    (name CHAR(20) NOT NULL, occupation VARCHAR(50),
    FOREIGN KEY (name) REFERENCES dramatis_personae
        ON DELETE CASCADE);
```

then:

```
DELETE FROM dramatis_personae WHERE name = 'Macbeth';
```

would delete all records about Macbeth from *both* tables. (See p. 19.)

# Data Control Language (DCL)

The DCL commands *GRANT* and *REVOKE* control security and access to data.

### GRANT

```
Syntax: GRANT privilege [, ...] ON [TABLE] table_name
        TO {user_id [, ...] | PUBLIC};
```

*GRANT* assigns privileges. A privilege is an authorization to perform an act. The most common privileges are  permission to *INSERT* into a given table, permission to *UPDATE* a given table, permission to *DELETE* from a given table, and permission to *SELECT* from a given table. A user may execute only those SQL commands which he or she has been granted, either explicitly (via a *GRANT* statement) or implicitly (because he or she created an object, for example the *dramatis_personae* table).

Privilege(s) are granted to specific users. A user is a person (identified by some *user_id* in the form of a string) who has access to the database. Sometimes privileges are granted to everybody, that is, to the *PUBLIC* at large.

Example: Suppose user *TRUDY* is the person who created the *dramatis_personae* table. This gives her the automatic right to perform all permissible operations on the table, including the right to grant privileges on it. She wants to assign the job of entering new records into *dramatis_personae* to user *PETER,* so must grant him permission to do so:

```
GRANT INSERT ON dramatis_personae TO PETER;
```

Once the data's in, she wants everyone who accesses the database to be able to *SELECT* from the table:

```
GRANT SELECT ON dramatis_personae TO PUBLIC;
```

### REVOKE

```
Syntax: REVOKE privilege [, ...] ON [TABLE] table-name
        FROM {user_id [, ...] | PUBLIC};
```

Suppose *TRUDY* fears that *PETER* will try to slip an unauthorized player into the *dramatis_personae* table. To prevent this, she cancels his permission to do *INSERT* with:

```
REVOKE INSERT ON dramatis_personae FROM PETER;
```

## Onward

The examples and descriptions in this chapter have been whirlwindish by design. We have tried to be brief, but still thorough enough to prepare you for the lessons that follow:

☐ how to embed SQL in C;

☐ how to implement the ODBC interface;

☐ how to optimize SQL performance.

If you've understood most of what we've touched on, you have what you need to proceed.

# Chapter 3

# Embedded Static SQL

Embedded SQL statements are SQL statements that occur within a program written in some other programming language (known as the host language). Such programs use SQL statements instead of routines written in the host language to carry out database operations. Embedded *static* SQL statements are fully known, and coded, when the program is written. Executing the program does not change them. (Embedded *dynamic* SQL statements, discussed in Chapter 4, are partially generated during execution.)

You can embed any SQL statement in a C program by preceding it with the words *exec sql* and terminating it with a semicolon. The SQL syntax rules described in Chapter 2 also apply to embedded SQL. In this chapter, we will address the other special tools you will need when invoking SQL from within a host language program.

Here are some examples of embedded static SQL commands:

```
exec sql create table table1 (column1 char(12));
exec sql insert into table1 values ('Hello world');
exec sql update table1 set column1 = 'Goodby world';
```

Since your C compiler won't recognize embedded SQL statements, an intermediary program (known as a precompiler) must translate them into C procedure calls before compiling and linking to an SQL DBMS library. Figure 3.1 shows the algorithm for a simple precompiler.

The precompiler will take this program:

```
void main ()
{
exec sql connect to database;
}
```

and change it to:

```
void main ()
{
procedure_name("connect to database");
}
```

which is a program your C compiler can process. (It will even link, assuming that the precompiler vendor supplied a library with a public routine called *procedure_name*.)

We'll call the library that actually executes the SQL commands in a program the SQL engine, and the precompiled C program that calls the engine the call-level SQL program. In embedded SQL programming then, the precompiler translates the embedded SQL source program into a call-level SQL program which, once compiled, can invoke the SQL engine via an Application Programming Interface (API).

```
open (input) embedded-SQL file
open (output) call-level-SQL file
pointer1 = * (next occurrence of the words 'exec sql')
pointer2 = * (next occurrence of the terminator ';')
string = (everything between pointer1 and pointer2)
output everything before pointer1
output 'procedure_name (', quote mark, string, quote mark, ');'
output everything after pointer2
close embedded-SQL file
close call-level-SQL file
```

**Figure 3.1**   *Algorithm for a simple precompiler.*

Chapter 5 will discuss how to program directly via the API using the most famous API specification — Microsoft's Open Database Connectivity (ODBC).

## *A Simple Example*

Here is a simple embedded SQL program:

```
/* PROGRAM PROGRAM1 */
void main ()
{
exec sql connect to database;
exec sql insert into table1 values ('Hello world');
}
```

In *PROGRAM1* the instruction:

```
exec sql connect to database;
```

tells the SQL engine what database we're working with — *database* is the name of the database in this case. Just as in C, where we have to open a file before we can read from it, in SQL we have to open a database before we can access it.

The program is not using standard SQL syntax because the ANSI SQL standard does not define how to open a database. This means that every SQL vendor must decide on the syntax for this task individually. Here is a sampling of the connection methods we've seen:

```
sqlestrd("database","password",'S',&sqlca); /* IBM OS/2
                                                data manager  */
/* nothing at all, just assume a default */ /* IBM DB2      */
dbuse(&loginrecord,"");                      /* Sybase       */
set database                                 /* XDB          */
SQLConnect(...);                             /* ODBC         */
exec sql connect to database;                /* Oracle/Ocelot */
```

But don't worry: SQL's details are well-defined. It's only the essential prerequisites that nobody can agree on. In this book, we'll always use:

```
exec sql connect to database;
```

to connect.

## *Exception Handling*

So far, *PROGRAM1* doesn't provide any feedback on whether or not the embedded SQL statements were successfully executed. To provide such information, the ANSI SQL standard specifies that, after the execution of each SQL statement in a program, a *status code* from the DBMS is to be placed in either or both of two special parameters called *sqlcode* and *SQLSTATE*. Using the status code, the host program can "find out" if the SQL statement was successful and react to an exception by printing a message or entering a remedial command path. *SQLSTATE* is the parameter preferred by ANSI SQL 92, but we'll also discuss *sqlcode* since many DBMSs still support its use.

# *"Hello World" in Embedded Static SQL*

Kernighan & Ritchie's *The C Programming Language* is a classic. We attribute this high regard to the clever way they started with a simple program at the beginning of Chapter 1:

```
main ()
{
        printf("hello world\n");
}
```

and gradually built on that foundation, not losing their readers till the appendices.

We want to stand on the shoulders of those giants, so we'll start this chapter with the simplest possible SQL program, and then add the complexity — which is mostly a matter of "how does the SQL DBMS get stuff from the host, i.e., the C, program, and how does the C program pass it back?" — as we go along. We'll divide our examples into specific, self-contained subsections, each one dealing with a separate matter of note in embedded SQL programming.

# The SQLCA

*sqlcode* resides within the SQLCA (SQL Communications Area). The SQLCA is a fixed size data structure that is used to show the completion status of embedded SQL statements. The SQLCA is updated by the SQL engine after the execution of every SQL statement (and therefore only contains information on the last SQL statement executed; each return from the DBMS overwrites the status code from the previous return). An application program containing executable SQL statements (any except *declare*, *include*, and *whenever*) should provide one SQLCA.

In C, the SQLCA can be defined globally. The SQLCA normally contains at least two variables. The first variable is an integer named *sqlcode* which will be set to 0 (zero) if the SQL statement executed correctly; to a value less than 0 if there was an error in executing the SQL statement; and to a value greater than 0 if the execution generated a warning. With the exception of *sqlcode==0* and one other exception, *sqlcode* values are not standardized by the ANSI SQL standard. The other exception is that a value of *100* means no more rows were found meeting the SQL statement's requirements. The second variable is a string which is set to a text message describing the *sqlcode* generated. The name of the string variable varies with different SQL vendors.

You can either define these variables yourself or use the embedded SQL instruction:

```
exec sql include sqlca;
```

which is supported by most SQL packages. The precompiler will translate this statement into something very similar to the following declaration:

```
int sqlcode;
char sqlmess_[255];
```

If your SQL package complies with SQL 92, then *sqlcode* will be named *SQLCODE* and will be defined as *long* rather than *int*.

A recent alternative to declaring an SQLCA is to declare *SQLSTATE* instead. *SQLSTATE* is a *char* variable with length *6* (the *SQLSTATE* status code is a five-character string; allow for \0 after it):

```
char SQLSTATE[6];
```

*SQLSTATE* values have mostly been standardized in SQL 92, and consist of a two-character class value followed by a three-character subclass value, made up of a combination of digits and upper case letters. Class code *00* means that the SQL statement executed correctly (the subclass code for "OK" is *000*, thus an *SQLSTATE* of *00000* equates with an *sqlcode* of *0*); class code *01* means that the execution generated a warning of some sort; and class code *02* means that no more rows were found meeting the SQL statement's requirements (an *SQLSTATE* of *02000* equates with an *sqlcode* of *100*).

Since *SQLSTATE* is in ODBC (see Chapter 5), it is becoming the preferred method for handling exceptions, and SQL 92 indicates that *sqlcode* is a deprecated feature. However, many DBMS packages, especially those with limited ODBC support, still use *sqlcode* exclusively, and therefore so will we in our chapters on embedded SQL, deferring use of *SQLSTATE* until our chapter on ODBC.

The following program demonstrates how to use an SQLCA to get status code feedback from the SQL engine:

```
exec sql include sqlca;
void main ()
{
exec sql connect to database;
exec sql insert into table1 values ('Hello world');
printf("The engine returned sqlcode =%d.\n",sqlcode);
printf("The engine returned this error message =%s.\n",sqlmess_);
}
```

Assuming the database contains a table named *table1*, the program provides feedback in the form of a message similar to this:

```
The engine returned sqlcode = 0.
The engine returned this error message = OK.
```

This tells us that the *insert* was successfully executed. If there is no table *table1* in the database the message from the DBMS would instead be something like this:

```
The engine returned sqlcode = -204.
The engine returned this error message = <table1> is an undefined name.
```

which tells us that *table1* hasn't been created and therefore our *insert* failed. Suppose we want the program to react to a non-existent *table1* by creating *table1* and attempting the *insert* again. Keeping in mind that all error returns from the DBMS will return a negative integer to *sqlcode*, we write:

```
exec sql include sqlca;
void main ()
{
exec sql connect to database;
exec sql insert into table1 values ('Hello world'); /*first insert*/

if (sqlcode<0) {
    exec sql create table table1 (s1 char(12));
    exec sql insert into table1 values ('Hello world');
}
printf("The engine returned sqlcode =%d.\n",sqlcode);
printf("The engine returned this error message =%s.\n",sqlmess_);
}
```

With this change, if the first *insert* (the one right after *connect to database*) succeeds, our program skips straight to the *printf* statements and tells us it's finished. If the first *insert* fails (i.e., returns a value less than zero to *sqlcode*), our program will create *table1* and do the *insert* again before going to the *printf* statements. The decision process is, of course, invisible to us when we're running the program.

Suppose, however, that the SQL engine fails doing the *connect to database* or the *create table* ? We no longer have the *sqlcode* returned by those statements because the subsequent *insert* wipes it out. To solve this problem, we add an *sqlcode* check after every SQL statement:

```
exec sql include sqlca;
void main ()
{
exec sql connect to database;
if (sqlcode<0) goto finis;
exec sql insert into table1 values ('Hello world');
if (sqlcode<0) {
    exec sql create table table1 (s1 char(12));
    if (sqlcode<0) goto finis;
    exec sql insert into table1 values ('Hello world');
}
finis:
printf("The engine returned sqlcode =%d.\n",sqlcode);
printf("The engine returned this error message =%s.\n",sqlmess_);
}
```

This solution is fine for small programs, but for a large program we'd like a cleaner solution.

## *The* whenever *Statement*

The designers of SQL understood the tedium of putting *if (sqlcode<0)* after every SQL statement, so they provided an embedded exception declaration that instructs the precompiler to add status check statements to the program. The statement:

```
exec sql whenever sqlerror goto finis;
```

tells the precompiler to add the following line after every SQL statement appearing subsequent to it in the program:

```
if (sqlcode<0) goto finis;
```

(*finis* is a C label in this case.)

SQL statements are always affected by the closest preceding *whenever* declaration in a program. To turn off the *goto finis* directive given in the above command, we would add this statement to our program:

```
exec sql whenever sqlerror continue;
```

This directive tells the precompiler to stop inserting *if (sqlcode<0) goto finis;* so the program will execute whichever line it would normally come to next, even in the event of an error return from the DBMS. If you have no *whenever* statement in your program, SQL assumes an implied *exec sql whenever sqlerror continue;* .

The following program is, after precompilation, the same as the last one we illustrated, but the *whenever* statements make our embedded SQL source code a bit cleaner:

```
/* PROGRAM PROGRAM2 */
exec sql include sqlca;
exec sql whenever sqlerror goto finis;
void main ()
{
    exec sql connect to database;
    exec sql whenever sqlerror continue;
    exec sql insert into table1 values ('Hello world');
    if (sqlcode<0) {
    exec sql whenever sqlerror goto finis;
    exec sql create table table1 (s1 char(12));
    exec sql insert into table1 values ('Hello world');
    }
    finis:
printf("The engine returned sqlcode =%d.\n",sqlcode);
printf("The engine returned this error message =%s.\n",sqlmess_);
}
```

This program will move to *finis*, display an error message, and end if the *connect* fails. If the *connect* doesn't fail, the *whenever continue* directive ensures that if we need to create *table1*, the program will move to the *create table* statement. If the *create table* statement fails, the *whenever goto finis* directive, which is again in effect, will cause the program to move to *finis*, display an error message, and then end.

Otherwise, the program will do the *insert* and then move to *finis*, displaying the status code for the *insert* before ending.

*whenever* directives are useful for catching problems in embedded SQL programs. Be warned, however: the major thing to remember about *whenever* is that *every* SQL statement following it is affected by it unless it is superseded by another *whenever*. This means that statements like `if (sqlcode<0) continue;` will be ignored even if you place them immediately after an SQL statement that follows *exec sql whenever sqlerror goto finis;*. This happens, for example, in the following bit of code:

```
exec sql include sqlca;
exec sql whenever sqlerror goto finis;        /* line #2 */
void main ()
{
    exec sql connect to database;
    exec sql insert into table1 values ('Hello world');
    if (sqlcode<0) {                           /* line #7 */
        exec sql create table table1 (s1 char(12)); }
    finis:
}
```

Line #7, `if (sqlcode<0) {`, will never be executed because the precompiler will insert `if (sqlcode<0) goto finis;` right after the *insert*, since the *insert* is still affected by the *whenever* statement at line #2.

We're at the point where *PROGRAM2* will successfully insert '*Hello world*' into *table1*. We therefore have only one more thing to consider before calling the program complete, and that is: Is *commit* automatic?

## Commit

All SQL updating instructions (which in this case means *update*, *delete*, or *insert* statements) can be completely canceled with *rollback* unless the changes have been made permanent with *commit*. With many SQL engines, the *commit* is implicit; that is, unless you set a special flag there's an automatic hidden *commit* after each updating instruction. But why depend on that? The flag might be off. Or the SQL engine you're using might assume that *rollback* is automatic. If you want your changes to be permanent, we recommend you eventually follow embedded SQL updating instructions with an explicit *commit*.

Here is *PROGRAM2* with a *commit* statement following the *insert*. Note that we are making another housekeeping change, as well. Instead of trying the *insert* first and creating *table1* if we need it, we will do the *create table* at the start of the program. If *table1* is already there, then that's fine — it won't be created again. We'll just make sure that if this is the case, we won't jump to *finis*. (Notice that the *commit* won't occur if the *insert* fails for some reason, because the *exec sql whenever sqlerror goto finis;* is in effect):

```
exec sql include sqlca;
exec sql whenever sqlerror goto finis;
void main ()
{
    exec sql connect to database;
    exec sql whenever sqlerror continue;
    exec sql create table table1 (s1 char(12));
    exec sql whenever sqlerror goto finis;
    exec sql insert into table1 values ('Hello world');
    exec sql commit;
    finis:
printf("The engine returned sqlcode =%d.\n",sqlcode);
printf("The engine returned this error message =%s.\n",sqlmess_);
}
```

Our program is now complete. We can take it to a customer and say, "Here is a C program containing embedded static SQL statements that will insert a value into a table."

# Passing Host Variables to SQL

A finicky customer might say, "But I don't want to put the words '*Hello world*' into the database. I want your program to ask me for two values at runtime. I'll type them in, and the values that I type are what you must insert into the table." Because SQL has no facility for keyboard input, to handle this request, C will have to accept the client's values and then pass them to SQL in variables instead of as constants. Since the variables are defined in the host language (that is, they are C variables), we call them *host variables*, and here is our program with the necessary modifications:

```
exec sql include sqlca;
exec sql whenever sqlerror goto finis;
exec sql begin declare section;
     char hostvariable1[13];
     char hostvariable2[3];
exec sql end declare section;
void main ()
{
exec sql connect to database;
exec sql whenever sqlerror continue;
exec sql create table table1 (s1 char(12), s2 char(2));
exec sql whenever sqlerror goto finis;
printf("Please type in first value.\n");
gets(hostvariable1);
printf("Please type in second value.\n");
gets(hostvariable2);
exec sql insert into table1 values (:hostvariable1, :hostvariable2);
exec sql commit;
finis:
printf("The engine returned sqlcode =%d.\n",sqlcode);
printf("The engine returned this error message =%s.\n",sqlmess_);
}
```

Host variables are variables defined according to the rules of the host language and used in embedded SQL statements to pass information between the database and the application program. When referring to host variables within an SQL statement, preface them with a colon, as we show in our *insert* statement.

In this example, the input typed by the user is assigned to the C string variables *hostvariable1* and *hostvariable2*.

These same variables — each with a colon preceding its name so the precompiler knows it's dealing with host variables instead of constants — are then placed as arguments in *exec sql insert*.

If, then, our user types the values *hello bob* and *hi*, in response to the prompts, the SQL engine processes the following SQL statement:

```
exec sql insert into table1 values ('hello bob', 'hi');
```

Host variables must be defined within an embedded declare section, delimited by the *exec sql begin declare section;* and *exec sql end declare section;* statements, as shown. These statements are, once again, precompiler directives. They signal the precompiler that host variable declarations are coming. We give the precompiler these signals because we assume it's stupid: it doesn't understand much about C syntax, so its only safe bet is to search the input file till it finds *exec sql*, and it won't try to parse anything outside a declare section block.

For numeric host variables, *long* defines an exact numeric variable whose SQL equivalent is *integer*; *int* defines an exact numeric variable whose SQL equivalent is *smallint*; *float* defines an approximate numeric variable whose SQL equivalent is *real*; and *double* defines an approximate numeric variable whose SQL equivalent is *double precision*.

For string host variables, *char* defines a string whose SQL equivalent is either *char* or *varchar*. The value in a *char* host variable is terminated by a null character and the position occupied by this null character must be included in the length of the host variable, so the equivalent SQL data type is *char* or *varchar*, with a defined length that is one less than the defined length of the C variable. The null terminator is not stored.

Thus, our program now contains the C variable declarations:

```
char hostvariable1[13];
char hostvariable2[3];
```

which equate with the SQL column definitions of *table1*:

```
s1 char(12), s2 char(2)
```

In C, *hostvariable1* and *hostvariable2* have been defined as 13 bytes and three bytes long, respectively, because we have to take the strings' trailing

\0 into account; thus, the values actually passed to the database will be only 12 bytes and two bytes long, respectively.

When we get to the *exec sql insert ... (:hostvariable1, :hostvariable2);* statement, we can see why the precompiler had to parse the host variable declarations earlier — because when it generates a C procedure, it has to know the host variable's type. In our example, if it had seen *int* in the declare section block, for instance, it would know that the engine will have to do an integer-to-string conversion before inserting the value.

The result of the precompilation, then, will be something like:

```
parameter_pass(hostvariable1,"null-terminated string");
parameter_pass(hostvariable2, "null-terminated string");
/* reminder: hostvariable1 and hostvariable2 are being passed by address */
procedure_call("insert into table1 values (?,?)");
```

The "?" in *procedure_call* means, by convention, "Use the host variable whose address you got in the last parameter-pass."

The host variable trick is useful because you can define as many host variables as you need, and you can use a host variable to replace any constant in an SQL statement, i.e.:

☐ in an *update* or *delete where* clause as a value to be compared;

☐ in an *update set* clause, as the source for an updated value;

☐ in an *insert values* clause, as the source for an inserted value;

☐ as an element of an arithmetic expression in a *set* or *where* clause, where the expression evaluates to a value to be retrieved, compared, or updated.

For example, after the *insert* we could put:

```
exec sql update table1 set s1 = 'goodbye world'
                                where s1< :hostvariable1;
exec sql update table1 set s1 = :hostvariable1;
exec sql delete from table1 where s1 = :hostvariable1;
```

So, the finicky customer can now enter new records into the database by entering input at a terminal. Naturally, the next step is that she will want to retrieve the data again.

# *Passing SQL Values to C*

You can also use host variables to pass values from SQL to C. To do so, you can replace literals in SQL statements as follows:

☐ in a *select* or *fetch into* clause, as the target for a retrieved value;

☐ in a *select where* clause as a value to be compared; and

☐ as an element of an arithmetic expression in a *select* clause, where the expression evaluates to a value to be retrieved, compared, or updated.

If the table you are retrieving from has only one row that matches your search criteria (such as the *hello bob* table created in the previous section), your program can employ what is known as a *singleton select* to get the values from SQL. For instance, this example will return the values *hello bob* and *hi* from *table1*:

```
exec sql select s1, s2 into :hostvariable1, :hostvariable2
                            from table1 where s1='hello bob';
printf("The value of s1 is: %s.\n",hostvariable1);
printf("The value of s2 is: %s.\n",hostvariable2);
```

This works because there is only one row in *table1* that matches the condition specified in the *where* clause. A singleton select is used to retrieve one specific row of data from a database. The value of the first column specified in the *select* is written to the first host variable named in the *into* clause; the value of the second column is written to the second host variable; and so on.

If more than one row can satisfy the retrieval conditions, a singleton select should not be used because it doesn't provide any mechanism for returning more than the first matching row to the host program. Some database packages even treat the use of a singleton select in such a case as an error and will not return any values to the host variables; others merely return the values from the first row found and stop.

To solve this problem, it would be neat if we could declare an array, *char hostvariable[n][13];* and let the *select* fill the array, but *n* could be an impossibly large number. So the general solution is to bring in the host variables from the database one row at a time by splitting the *select* into separate steps (declare cursor, open curson, fetch cursor, and close cursor), using an SQL object called the *cursor.*

A cursor is an object that provides the host language program with a mechanism for individually processing each of a set of rows retrieved from a database. The cursor can be thought of as a kind of pointer which can be moved through a set of rows, providing the program with access to each row separately.

To understand the role of a cursor, assume the SQL engine builds a results table to hold all the rows retrieved by a *select* statement executed in an application program. The engine uses a cursor to make the rows of the results table available to the program. The cursor identifies, or points to, the current row of the results table (see Figure 3.2).

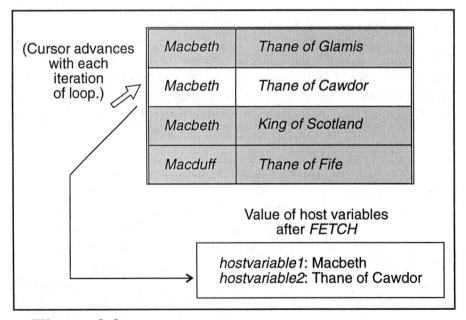

**Figure 3.2**    *The SQL cursor points to a row of the results table. That row is then available for a* fetch. *Using a cursor and a loop routine, the host program can extract an entire multi-row select.*

A cursor is always associated with a specific *select* statement through a *declare cursor* declaration. You can make this declaration anytime before the first use of the cursor. Since the declaration doesn't actually process the *select*, you can even declare the cursor before setting the values of any host variables associated with it.

The *open* statement processes the declared *select*, and it is at this point that the values of the host variables are set. (Changing the values of the host variables after the cursor has been opened, and before it has been closed again, has no effect on the results table.) After *open*, all the rows matching the search criteria have been retrieved. As long as the cursor is open, it is associated with this specific set of rows. *open* positions the cursor prior to the first row of the results table.

Each time it is called, the *fetch* statement moves the cursor to the next row of the results table and writes the values from that row into a set of host variables. If your DBMS supports SQL 92, you can declare a *scroll cursor* which can be scrolled (think of a scroll bar) up to fetch the first row, down to fetch the next or the last row, and back and forth within the results table to fetch a prior or following row (or a row at an absolute or relative position in the results table). With a non-scrollable cursor, only *fetch next* is possible.

Finally, the *close* statement deactivates the cursor. If another *open* reactivates the cursor later in the program, the SQL engine will retrieve a new results table based on the host variable and database values at that time. In the meantime, attempts to *fetch* from or *close* the cursor will fail.

This example declares a cursor called *FROM_TAB1* and uses it to pass data from *table1* to the host variables *hostvariable1* and *hostvariable2*:

```
exec sql declare FROM_TAB1 cursor for select s1, s2 from table1;
exec sql open FROM_TAB1;
for (;;) {
        exec sql fetch FROM_TAB1 into :hostvariable1, :hostvariable2;
        printf("The value of s1 is: %s.\n",hostvariable1);
        printf("The value of s2 is: %s.\n",hostvariable2); }
exec sql close FROM_TAB1;
```

Since the table does not have an infinite number of rows, we'd like to break out of the *fetch* loop when we hit the end of the set. Once again, SQL's designers have anticipated this need. The ANSI SQL standard specifies that *sqlcode* will be set to +100 when there are no more rows to fetch, so we can write:

```
exec sql declare FROM_TAB1 cursor for select s1, s2 from table1;
exec sql open FROM_TAB1;
for (;;) {
        exec sql fetch FROM_TAB1 into :hostvariable1, :hostvariable2;
        if (sqlcode==100) break;
        printf("The value of s1 is: %s.\n",hostvariable1);
        printf("The value of s2 is: %s.\n",hostvariable2); }
exec sql close FROM_TAB1;
```

You can also use the *whenever* statement to provide an escape from the *fetch* loop:

```
exec sql whenever not found goto <label>;
```

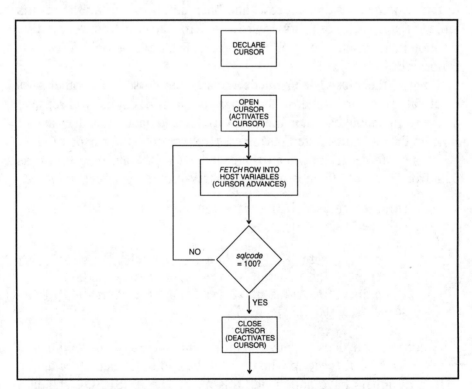

**Figure 3.3** *The DOFLEC procedure allows the host program to extract the result of a multi-row* select.

results in the precompiler inserting:

```
if (sqlcode==100) goto <label>;
```

after every executable SQL statement. As with *whenever sqlerror*, this can be turned off again with:

```
exec sql whenever not found continue;
```

The following program uses a cursor to *select* from the database and prints the result:

```
exec sql include sqlca;
exec sql whenever sqlerror goto finis1;
exec sql whenever not found goto finis2;
exec sql begin declare section;
     char hostvariable1[13];
     char hostvariable2[3];
 exec sql end declare section;
void main()
{
exec sql connect to database;
exec sql declare FROM_TAB1 cursor for select s1,s2 from table1;
exec sql open FROM_TAB1;
for(;;) {
     exec sql fetch FROM_TAB1 into :hostvariable1,:hostvariable2;
     printf("The value of s1 is: %s.\n",hostvariable1);
     printf("The value of s2 is: %s.\n",hostvariable2); }
finis2:
exec sql close FROM_TAB1;
printf("All rows retrieved\n");
finis1:
printf("The engine returned sqlcode =%d.\n",sqlcode);
printf("The engine returned this error message = %s.\n",sqlmess_);
}
```

In one form or another, this Declare + Open + Fetch-Loop-till-End-of-set + Close procedure appears in all serious SQL programs every time data has to flow from the database to the host (see Figure 3.3). Taking the first initials, you have the mnemonic "DOFLEC." If you remember DOFLEC, you know how to use SQL cursors.

# NULL *Values & Indicator Variables*

As we said in Chapter 2, SQL represents missing information with *NULL*s. Although we often call this the *NULL* value and speak of a column containing *NULL*s, it is important to remember that the whole point about *NULL*s is that they are *not* values. Instead, they are markers, showing where precise information is missing from the database. Thus, *NULL* is a special marker used to represent "value unknown" or "value inapplicable." *NULL* is not the same as a blank or a zero.

If we want to insert an SQL *NULL* into a table, we're going to have some trouble with our C host program because C doesn't know what *NULL*s are. We can't just say:

```
strcpy(hostvariable,"NULL");
exec sql insert into table1 (s1) values (:hostvariable);
```

because SQL will cheerily insert the four-character, non-*NULL* word *NULL* into the table.

We might think that this syntax has a chance:

```
strcpy(hostvariable,"");
exec sql insert into table1 (s1) values (:hostvariable);
```

Weirdly enough, this works — with Oracle. But most systems will, quite rightly, take it that you're trying to insert a blank. *NULL*s in SQL are unrelated to nulls in C. They aren't blanks, they are not \Øs, and in fact they cannot be represented with any combination of ASCII characters.

The correct way to pass a *NULL*, then, is to pass it using two variables: the host variable itself, and an *indicator variable*, which is normally defined as an integer. (The ANSI SQL standard specifies that an indicator must be defined as exact numeric with a scale of zero.) The indicator variable is set to a specific value which tells us whether or not the value passed to or from the associated host variable was *NULL*. (In the first case, passing a *NULL* to the database via a host variable, the indicator must be set to *-1* by the host program. In the second case, passing a *NULL* from the database to a host variable, the DBMS sets the indicator to *-1*.)

When a host variable is passed to the database and its associated indicator variable is set to *-1*, the SQL engine interprets this as meaning "the host is passing me a *NULL*." Otherwise the SQL engine knows the host is simply passing the value of the host variable. The *insert* statement looks like this:

```
exec sql insert into table1 (s1) values (:hostvariable :indicator);
```

or, in correct ANSI syntax:

```
exec sql insert into table1 (s1)
   values (:hostvariable INDICATOR :indicator);
```

There is an alternative to using indicator variables to insert *NULL*s into a database. The statement:

```
exec sql insert into table1 (s1) values (NULL);
```

will also do the job, as will forcing the insertion of a default *NULL* value into a column by omitting it from an *insert* statement. For example:

```
exec sql create table2 (s1 integer, s2 char(12));
exec sql insert into table2 (s2) values ('Boston');
```

The *insert* shown above will put a *NULL* into column *s1*, since it wasn't given a specific value to insert into the column.

Once a row of data contains one or more *NULL*s, there is a corresponding problem when retrieving that row. Again, application programs must prepare for receiving *NULL*s from the database by associating an indicator variable with any host variable that can receive a *NULL*. Now that many DBMSs support at least some form of outer join, even if there are no rows with *NULL*s anywhere in the database — indeed, even if all columns are declared as *NOT NULL* columns — your SQL engine can still return *NULL*s either from a *select* that contains an outer join or with the (non-ANSI) *select NULL from table;* statement. To be on the safe side, always couple your host variables with indicator variables when moving data from the database to the host.

When data is passed to a host variable from the database and its associated indicator variable is set to *-1* by the DBMS, the host program interprets this as meaning "the database is passing me a *NULL*." When this happens, most DBMSs just change the value of the indicator variable — they do not write anything to the host variable at all. A host variable can thus sometimes contain a leftover value from a previous *fetch*. You should be prepared to re-initialize or ignore the host variable in case this happens.

The following example shows our *select* program with an indicator variable:

```
exec sql include sqlca;
exec sql whenever sqlerror goto finis1;
exec sql whenever not found goto finis2;
exec sql begin declare section;
    char hostvariable[13];
    int indicator;
exec sql end declare section;
void main ()
{
    exec sql connect to database;
    exec sql declare FROM_TAB1 cursor for select s1 from table1;
    exec sql open FROM_TAB1;
    for (;;) {
        exec sql fetch FROM_TAB1 into :hostvariable :indicator;
        if (indicator<0)
         {
         strcpy (hostvariable,"NULL");
         }
        printf("The value of s1 is: %s.\n",hostvariable);
            }
    finis2:
exec sql close FROM_TAB1;
printf("All rows retrieved\n");
    finis1:
printf("The engine returned sqlcode =%d.\n",sqlcode);
printf("The engine returned this error message: %s.\n",sqlmess_);
}
```

In this example, the instruction *if (indicator<0)* determines if the indicator variable is negative, indicating that the value being returned from the database is a *NULL*.

Only if the indicator is >=0 can the program use the returned value of *hostvariable*, because if the indicator is negative, the value of *hostvariable* could be left over from a previous *fetch*. When this does happen, the program places the character string *NULL* into *hostvariable* so that we can see that the returned value was a *NULL*.

# *Summary: Embedded Static SQL*

Here is a summary of what you can do with embedded static SQL:

☐ You can mix, or embed, SQL statements into the source code of a host language, such as C, provided the SQL statements begin with *exec sql* and end with a semicolon.

☐ You can specify where the status code for each SQL statement executed will be put by placing the SQL statement:

```
exec sql include sqlca;
```

or the C variable declaration:

```
char SQLSTATE[6];
```

at the start of the program. The first declaration provides you with status code information in the integer, *sqlcode*. The second declaration provides you with status code information in the string, *SQLSTATE*. The program can use these variables to test for errors, either with:

```
if (sqlcode<0)
```

or with:

```
if (strcmp(SQLSTATE,"02000")>0)
```

(Caution: In many systems, *sqlcode* is part of a structure, so the test would look something like "*if (sqlca.sqlcode<0)*".) The program can also use these variables to test for an end-of-fetch-loop, either with:

```
if (sqlcode==100)
```

or with:

```
if (strcmp(SQLSTATE,"02000")==0)
```

☐ You can give directives to the precompiler —

```
exec sql whenever sqlerror goto <label>;
exec sql whenever sqlerror continue;
exec sql whenever not found goto <label>;
exec sql whenever not found continue;
```

which can simplify exception condition checking.

☐ You can define host variables within the program and use them to pass data between the host and the database by placing them in SQL statements (with their names preceded by a colon) wherever a literal would otherwise occur. Host variables used this way should be declared within the following pair of statements:

```
exec sql begin declare section;
exec sql end declare section;
```

☐ You can pass data from SQL to the host using singleton selects (if only one row will match the retrieval criteria) or DOFLECs (for multiple row retrieval).

☐ You can use an indicator to specify whether a host variable should in fact be interpreted as having no known value — that is, as *NULL*.

In short, you can now write an adequate application program using embedded static SQL.

"But," you might say, "in real world applications, what you've shown me so far isn't enough. How do I handle situations where the exact type, size, and number of variables isn't known ahead of time?"

For the answer, read on!

# *Embedded Dynamic SQL*

Suppose your program requirements look like this:

> "There is no restriction on operator input. The client can type
> in any SQL statement at all and get an appropriate answer."

If your resources were limited to the SQL we've described so far, you wouldn't be able to fulfill this demand because the operations your programs can perform are fixed at precompile time. That's why what we've seen so far is called static SQL. Static SQL statements are fully known when the application program is written. Although they allow the program a fair amount of flexibility through the use of host variables, they are still limited to what the designer anticipated when writing the program.

In contrast, dynamic SQL statements allow a program to handle user requests without knowing in advance exactly what those requests are going to be.

A useful analogy is C's distinguishment of static and dynamic for memory allocation, as seen in the following C code:

```
char x[1000];            /* 1000-byte static memory allocation  */
void main()
{
    char*y;
    y=(char*)malloc(1000); /* 1000-byte dynamic memory allocation */
}
```

To process most SQL statements dynamically, a program must be able to accept a string containing the SQL statement, then parse and execute the string *at runtime*. SQL's designers have provided a way to do this.

## *The* execute immediate *Statement*

```
/* PROGRAM — ADHOC.C */
exec sql include sqlca;
exec sql begin declare section;
    char hostvariable1[255];
exec sql end declare section;
void main ()
{
    exec sql connect to database;
    for (;;) {
        printf("Type in any string, or <cr> to exit.\n");
        gets(hostvariable1);
        if (strlen(hostvariable1)==0) exit(0);
        exec sql execute :hostvariable1; /* 'execute' statement */
        if (sqlcode>=0) printf("OK.\n");
        else printf("Error. sqlcode=%d.\n",sqlcode); }
}
```

The SQL *execute* statement allows the ADHOC.C program to process most executable SQL statements dynamically. Rather than embedding the statement into the program code, simply assign it to a host language string variable which the program will reference through an *execute* command.

In the above example, the *execute* statement's argument is the C string *hostvariable1*, to which the user's input is assigned. When the program reaches *execute*, it processes this string and returns error information on the executed statement to the SQLCA, just as the commands in the last chapter did.

Any SQL statement can be assigned to *hostvariable1* except: *begin declare section, end declare section, declare cursor, open, fetch, close, describe, execute, include sqlca, include sqlda, select*, and *whenever* — all of which are considered non-executable for this purpose. (Note that in this context, "executable SQL statement" means one which can be dynamically processed by the *execute* statement. This is different from the normal interpretation of the word.) The assigned string may not contain the words *exec sql* or a terminating semicolon.

Notice that the code still contains many of the same SQL statements used in Chapter 3. Error handling with *whenever* and *include sqlca*, host variables, and indicator variables are also needed in dynamic SQL programs.

Here, for instance, is a sample session of *ADHOC.C* (with the computer's prompts in bold type):

```
C:\> adhoc <cr>
```
**Type in any string, or <cr> to exit:**
```
connect to database; <cr>
```
**OK.**
**Type in any string, or <cr> to exit:**
```
create table t (col1 integer); <cr>
```
**OK.**
**Type in any string, or <cr> to exit:**
```
insert into t (col1) values (1000); <cr>
```
**OK.**
**Type in any string, or <cr> to exit:**
```
alter table t add col2 char(50); <cr>
```
**OK.**
**Type in any string, or <cr> to exit:**
```
update t set col2='Lady Macbeth'; <cr>
```
**OK.**
**Type in any string, or <cr> to exit:**
```
create index aind on t (col2); <cr>
```
**OK.**
**Type in any string, or <cr> to exit:**
```
commit; <cr>
```

> **OK.**
> **Type in any string, or <cr> to exit:**
> **<cr>**
> **C:\>**

This form of the *execute* command is also known as *execute immediate*, because the SQL statement assigned to its argument may not contain any host variables — the argument must be ready to execute without requiring additional information.

## execute ... using

*execute* also has an optional *using* clause that allows for the dynamic input of host variables in *execut)e*'s argument string. Rather than putting a host variable in the SQL statement assigned to the argument, put a parameter marker (denoted by a question mark) in the statement instead. When the statement is executed, the parameter marker is replaced with the contents of a host variable specified in the *using* clause.

To illustrate, suppose we assign the value *5* to a C integer variable called *hostvariable2* and the value *insert into table2 values (?)* to a C string called *hostvariable1*. The question mark in the *values* clause is the parameter marker that will be replaced with the value of a host variable specified in the *using* clause. Thus, the statement:

```
exec sql execute :hostvariable1 using :hostvariable2;
```

will actually transform at runtime into:

```
exec sql insert into table2 values (5);
```

The following program shows *execute ... using* in context. It creates a table and inserts the value of *hostvariable2* into the table dynamically. It then uses a singleton *select* to retrieve the value:

```
exec sql include sqlca;
exec sql whenever sqlerror goto finis;
exec sql begin declare section;
     char hostvariable1[255];
     int hostvariable2;
     int hostvariable3;
exec sql end declare section;
void main ()
{
     strcpy(hostvariable1,"insert into table2 values (?)");
     hostvariable2=5;
     hostvariable3=0
     exec sql connect to database;
     exec sql create table table2 (col1 smallint);
     exec sql execute :hostvariable1 using :hostvariable2;
     exec sql select col1 into :hostvariable3 from table2;
     printf("%d ",hostvariable3); exit(0);
     finis:
     printf("The engine returned sqlcode = %d.\n",sqlcode);
     printf("The engine returned this error message =%s.\n",sqlmess_);
}
```

This program will work with most SQL DBMSs but not with all of them. This is because the ANSI SQL standard, and many DBMS packages, add another step to this process by requiring that an SQL statement containing parameters be prepared before it is executed. This is done using the *prepare* statement, as follows:

```
strcpy (hostvariable1,"insert into table2 values (?)");
hostvariable2=5;
....
exec sql prepare prepped_statement from :hostvariable1;
exec sql execute prepped_statement using :hostvariable2;
```

Here, *prepare* prepares *prepped_statement* from *hostvariable1*. *execute* then executes *prepped_statement*, rather than *hostvariable1* as it did before.

The result of these statements is exactly the same as the result from the previous example — that is, the SQL statement actually executed is:

```
exec sql insert into table2 values (5);
```

Note that, since *prepped_statement* is an SQL object rather than a C host variable, you needn't declare it in a *declare section* or preface it with a colon in either the *prepare* or *execute* command.

# Dynamic vs. Static SQL

Dynamic SQL is more flexible and versatile than static SQL, but if you have a good precompiler, static SQL is much faster. Not only can a precompiler a) parse and check for syntax errors, it can b) ensure that tables exist, c) perform authorization checks, d) choose among varying optimal strategies for doing the same job, and even e) translate to pseudocode, which can lead to short cuts. (For instance, the pseudocode might contain the direct address of a table in the database catalog, so the SQL engine doesn't have to look up the address in a catalog index at runtime.)

A precompiler that performs tasks b) through e) is said to be *binding* the code with the database since the resultant code depends on what's in the database catalog. Since the precompiler can't get the information it needs for such tasks from the words *exec sql execute :string;*, in dynamic SQL all parsing and binding burdens are put off until runtime. This normally results in slower and bigger programs.

# Dynamic SQL Select

Suppose a client asks for an application program that will let her submit ad hoc queries to the database. "Nothing fancy," says she, "just display the result of each *select* on my terminal in tabular form, showing the column names as headings."

Such a program not only has to accept the client's input dynamically, it has to know (among other things) how many columns she's retrieving, plus the name, data type, size, and value of each column she's retrieving. How can the program prepare for a *select* without knowing what the question will be? The *execute* command can't process the client's input dynamically because *execute* won't know where to put the *select* result. The SQL engine will certainly understand the following:

```
exec sql begin declare section;
    char hostvariable[255]="select * from table1";
exec sql end declare section;
void main()
{
    exec sql connect to database;
    exec sql execute :hostvariable;
}
```

and can simply execute the legal SQL statement *select * from table1;* — But where does it put the result? The SQL engine doesn't care what the program wants to do with the data — display it, count the i's in it, write it to a file — but it *does* have to know where to put it, and *execute* has no mechanism for passing data back to the program.

The DOFLEC loop introduced in Chapter 3 is able to pass data to the program, and you could use it in combination with *execute* if you wanted to write a really quick and dirty bit of code as a temporary measure:

```
exec sql include sqlca;
exec sql whenever sqlerror goto finis;
exec sql begin declare section;
    char hostvariable[255]="select * from table1";
    char host_1[1000]="";
    char host_2[1000]="";
    char host_3[1000]="";
exec sql end declare section;
void main ()
{
    exec sql connect to database;
    exec sql declare FROM_TAB1 cursor for :hostvariable;
    exec sql open FROM_TAB1;
    for (;;) {
        exec sql fetch FROM_TAB1 into :host_1, :host_2, :host_3;
        if (sqlcode==100) break;
        printf("the value of the first column is: %s.\n",host_1);
        printf("the value of the second column is: %s.\n",host_2);
        printf("the value of the third column is: %s.\n",host_3); }
    exec sql close FROM_TAB1;
    finis:
    printf("The engine returned sqlcode = %d.\n",sqlcode);
    printf("The engine returned this error message =%s.\n",sqlmess_);
}
```

Here we've used the DOFLEC structure with *execute*, and we've specified host variables to store the results. The code will work, but it has some substantial drawbacks. This method gobbles RAM, increases in complexity if we allow for more columns, can't handle all cases (perhaps our DBMS can't convert integers to strings), and won't provide all the data we might need anyway.

Although dynamic SQL does provide access to a set of multiple rows by means of a cursor, the cursor's abilities shown in Chapter 3 are inadequate to process a dynamic *select*.

## *The SQLDA*

What we need is an additional mechanism that will accept a dynamic *select* as input and, after parsing it, return all pertinent information (number of columns, column names, data types, sizes, etc.) directly to the program. The same information then has to be made available to the DOFLEC loop. SQL provides a descriptor mechanism for this purpose.

The SQLDA (SQL Descriptor Area) is a set of variables set aside to receive information about a dynamic *select* result. This information is written to the SQLDA by the *describe* statement, which we will discuss later.

(NOTE: SQL 92 now provides a method of processing *select* dynamically using the new statements *allocate descriptor*, *deallocate descriptor*, *get descriptor*, *set descriptor*, and *describe*. We have chosen not to use this in our examples because most DBMSs on the market have been, and still are, doing the job with slightly different syntax.)

The SQLDA used by most DBMSs consists of a set of (usually four) variables describing the SQLDA itself, followed by a number of occurrences of an array of (usually five) variables, collectively named *sqlvar*, which collectively describe one column of the *select* result. Storage for the SQLDA is allocated dynamically by the application program.

The address of the allocated storage for each host variable associated with a dynamic *select*, as well as the variable's data type, size, and a pointer to its indicator variable, are all specified within the SQLDA.

The (non-ANSI) statement:

```
exec sql include sqlda;
```

is provided by most DBMSs to initialize a vendor-supplied SQLDA declaration. You can either embed this statement into the program or declare the SQLDA structure yourself. We'll use *exec sql include sqlda;* in our examples.

Figure 4.1 shows a typical SQLDA definition.

## describe

The *describe* statement assigns values to SQLDA's variables. Coupled with a DOFLEC loop that is slightly different from the one described in Chapter 3, *describe* and an SQLDA provide the mechanism needed to process a dynamic *select*. Here are the essential SQL statements:

```
exec sql include sqlda;
exec sql prepare prepped-statement from :select-statement;
exec sql describe prepped-statement into :descriptor-area;
exec sql declare cursor-name cursor for prepped-statement;
exec sql open cursor-name;
exec sql fetch cursor-name using descriptor :descriptor-area;
exec sql close cursor-name;
```

```
struct sqlda {
    char sqldaid[8];        /* "SQLDA   " - set by INCLUDE SQLDA          */
    long int sqldabc;       /* length of sqlda - set by INCLUDE SQLDA     */
    int sqln;               /* max sqlvar occurrences - set by INCLUDE SQLDA */
    int sqld;               /* current sqlvar occurrences - set by DESCRIBE */
    struct sqlvar {         /* defined sqln times, actually occurs sqld times */
        int sqltype;        /* type of column - set by DESCRIBE           */
        int sqllen;         /* size of column - set by DESCRIBE           */
        char far *sqldata;  /* pointer -> variable - programmer has to add */
        int far *sqlind;    /* pointer -> indicator - programmer has to add */
        struct sqlname {    /* string, up to 30 bytes long set by DESCRIBE */
            int length;     /* 1-word size of name - set by DESCRIBE      */
            char data[30]; } sqlname; } sqlvar[MV]; };
struct sqlda sqlda={"SQLDA",0,MV,0};
```

**Figure 4.1**   *The SQL Descriptor Area (SQLDA) usually consists of four variables describing the SQLDA itself, followed by multiple occurrences of a structure that contains the description of one column of a dynamic* select *result.*

When you embed these statements into a program, replace the syntactic categories identified by select-statement, descriptor-area, cursor-name, and prepped-statement with your own object names. Replace *select-statement* with the name of the C string variable that contains a dynamically input *select* command, replace *descriptor-area* with the name of the SQLDA structure (usually *sqlda*), replace *cursor-name* with the name of the cursor, and replace *prepped_statement* with the name of the prepared *select* statement string.

Note the differences between the syntax of the DOFLEC statements shown in Chapter 3 and those shown here. The first difference is that a dynamic *select* statement is not placed in the *declare cursor...for* clause. Instead, the *select* is assigned to a string host variable which is prepared by the *prepare* statement, and the prepared statement's name is put into *declare cursor*. The second difference is that the *fetch* statement has no *into* clause. Instead, it has a *using descriptor* clause, whose argument is the name of the same SQLDA to which the *describe* statement will assign values.

After the string containing the dynamic *select* has been prepared, *describe* uses the prepared statement to fill in the SQLDA structure (see Figure 4.1).

First, it writes the number of columns that will be retrieved into *sqlda.sqld*. Then, for each *sqlda.sqld* occurence, it fills *.sqlvar.sqllen* with the size of a column, *.sqlvar.sqltype* with a numeric code for the column's data type, and *.sqlname* with the size of the column name and the name itself. (The *sqlvar.sqltype* code numbers for the most common data types are shown in Figure 4.2. The *NOT NULL?* column indicates whether or not a column with the given data type is defined as *NOT NULL*. Thus, the number returned to *sqlvar.sqltype* is always odd if it is possible that the column's value could be *NULL*.)

Note that *describe* does not supply any addresses for the contents of the columns that will be retrieved. SQL's designers figured that this job requires some dynamic memory allocation, which is best left to the host language. (Memory allocation is troublesome in some host languages, but C has an easy time of it.)

Once *describe* is finished, the cursor declared for the prepared statement is opened, the *fetch* is performed using the information provided by the SQLDA, and the cursor is closed.

To illustrate, suppose that the string *select \* from table1* has been assigned to *:select-statement*, and that *table1*'s definition is *create table table1 (c1 char(12), c2 integer);*. You could display the column definitions with:

```
exec sql include sqlca;
exec sql include sqlda;
exec sql begin declare section;
     char hostvariable[]="select * from table1";
exec sql end declare section;
void main ()
{
    int i;
    struct sqlvar *varptr;
    exec sql connect to database;
    exec sql prepare PREPPED_STATEMENT from :hostvariable;
    exec sql describe PREPPED_STATEMENT into :sqlda;
    printf("There are %d columns.\n",sqlda.sqld);
    for (i=0; i<sqlda.sqld; ++i) {
        varptr=&sqlda.sqlvar[i];
```

| CODE | SQL DATA-TYPE | NOT NULL? |
|------|---------------|-----------|
| 384 | DATE | YES |
| 385 | DATE | NO |
| 388 | TIME | YES |
| 389 | TIME | NO |
| 392 | TIMESTAMP | YES |
| 393 | TIMESTAMP | NO |
| 448 | VARCHAR | YES |
| 449 | VARCHAR | NO |
| 452 | CHAR | YES |
| 453 | CHAR | NO |
| 480 | FLOAT | YES |
| 481 | FLOAT | NO |
| 484 | DECIMAL | YES |
| 485 | DECIMAL | NO |
| 496 | INTEGER | YES |
| 497 | INTEGER | NO |
| 500 | SMALLINT | YES |
| 501 | SMALLINT | NO |

**Figure 4.2**   *Code numbers for SQL data types.* describe *stores the type code number for each column of a dynamic select into* sqlvar.sqltype. *See Figure 4.1 for the components of* sqlvar.

```
        printf("Name of column %d is: %s.\n",i,varptr->sqlname.data);
        printf("Type of column %d is: %d.\n",i,varptr->sqltype);
        printf("Size of column %d is: %d.\n",i,varptr->sqllen); }
   }
```

## *Algorithm for a Dynamic* `select`

A dynamic *select* is one in which the number and types of columns to be retrieved aren't known when the application program is coded. Because of this, you will not know the number and types of host variables to assign the results to. Figure 4.3 shows the algorithm for a dynamic *select*.

## *An Example*

Listing 4.1 is a fairly large C program that uses embedded dynamic SQL. Its purpose is to provide an interactive interface for ad hoc SQL queries.

If you want to use dynamic SQL, code like the program shown in Listing 4.1 cannot be avoided or simplified in conventional C. But it isn't as daunting as it seems because, in its essentials, it's always the same. You do have to understand it because you'll have to change the details for specific situations, but Listing 4.1 can serve as a template, which we hope you will find useful.

## *A Wrap-up of Embedded SQL's Good and Bad Points*

So: you've got C and you've got SQL. You want to do something in C — loop control, input/output, interfacing to a GUI library? Go ahead. You want to do something in SQL — update or query a database? Fine too. You want to mix the two — putting SQL statements in a C loop, displaying what's in the database with a GUI? You can do that. When you leave C to do what it's good at, it blows away the "database languages." When you use SQL for what it does best, it blows away the ISAM libraries. You put C and SQL together, and, well, why would you want to do anything else?

But the subject of this book isn't whether C and SQL are beautiful by themselves, it's whether their *marriage* is beautiful. That is: Is embedded

1) Include an SQLCA in your program for SQL status return information:

```
exec sql include sqlca;
```

2) Declare an SQLDA structure to provide storage for information returned on the columns of a dynamic select:

```
exec sql include sqlda;
```

3) Declare a string host variable within a *declare* section and assign the *select* statement to it:

```
exec sql begin declare section;
    char hostvariable1[255];
exec sql end declare section;
    ....
printf("Input your query:\n");
gets(hostvariable1);
```

4) Prepare the *select* statement from the host variable:

```
exec sql prepare prepped_statement from :hostvariable1;
```

5) Describe the prepared statement into the SQLDA:

```
exec sql describe prepped_statement into :sqlda;
```

6) Declare a cursor for the prepared statement:

```
exec sql declare cursor_s cursor for prepped_statement;
```

7) Using C code instead of SQL, get information about the name, data type, and size of each column in the *select* result from the SQLDA. With this information, calculate the storage needed for one record and allocate it.

8) Open the cursor:

```
exec sql open cursor_s;
```

9) In a loop which operates on the *select* result, *fetch* the data one record at a time, using the information provided by the SQLDA:

```
exec sql fetch cursor_s using descriptor :sqlda;
```

10) Close the cursor:

```
exec sql close cursor_s;
```

11) Using C code, free the storage allocated in step 7.

**Figure 4.3**    *Algorithm for a dynamic* select.

SQL the best way to join C with SQL? Actually, this marriage has a few rocks.

First: embedding SQL in C obviously works, but it's just as obvious that this *exec sql* stuff wasn't designed with C in mind. (Hint: what wordy mainframe language do you think SQL was interfaced with first?)

Second: embedded SQL programs are only portable as source code. There is no way, for instance, to substitute a .*DLL* written with XDB's embedded SQL by simply plugging in one written with Oracle's because the binaries differ.

Third: the dynamic *selects* in particular are ugly.

Presumably as a result of these problems, only about half of all DBMS vendors offer precompilers and embedded SQL. Either as an option or as the only alternative, some vendors propose to the user that coding should be done at the lower, API level.

So maybe C programmers would prefer to directly use function calls rather than coding in embedded SQL and having the precompiler translate to an API. Since every vendor had a different API, this didn't matter much to those of us who care about standards: embedded SQL was the only choice. But now there's a good contender for an API standard. We'll cover it in the next chapter.

# Listing 4.1

```
/* Embedded-SQL C program for executing any SQL command 'online' with
MS-DOS*/

/* This program has one loop in main(), which prompts the user to type
in any SQL command. If the command is 'EXIT', the program exits the
loop and returns to MS-DOS. If the command is 'SELECT ...', the
program calls the doselect() procedure, and the user will see a
columnar display of the results. If the command is anything else,
the program simply executes the command and displays the returned
error information.

The program can run into these problems which are common to all
columnar-display scenarios:
1) not enough room on one line (solved by shrinking 'screen column'
     widths and allowing more than one line for each 'SQL row'),
2) not enough room on one page (solved by stopping at the end of an
     'SQL row' and prompting the user to hit a key to see more),
3) width of header greater than width of 'SQL column' (solved by
     allocating more lines for the header).

Implementation-specific notes: the assumed compiler is Borland C++
v3.1 (we use a few Borland-specific library routines). The assumed
DBMS is the one supplied with this book. Other SQL DBMSs may differ in
these ways:
a) they may require the use of EXEC SQL EXECUTE IMMEDIATE rather
     than EXEC SQL EXECUTE,
b) they may require the use of PREPARE (we've omitted this step),
c) they may be unable to convert all non-CHAR data to CHAR,
d) 'sqlcode' may be called 'sqlca.sqlcode', and 'sqlmess_' may
     either be absent or have another name.
Except for those minor differences, this program should work with
any and all 'embedded-SQL' database management systems.*/

/* The screen is divided into a command area, an error-information
display area, and a selected-columns display area. For example:*/

/* COMMAND: select author,title from book;          starts at LINE_1*/
/*                                                                  */
/* Error code = 0, "OK"                             starts at LINE_5*/
```

## Listing 4.1 — continued

```
/* AUTHOR      |    TITLE                    (header)       */
/* --------------------------------------                   */
/* Smith, J    |    My life in pictures      (body)         */
/* Smith, K    |    My life in sounds                       */
/* [Type any key to see next row]            this is LINE_LAST*/

#define     LINE_1          1
#define     LINE_5          5
#define     LINE_LAST       25

/* prototype of 'gotoxy', 'clreol', 'clrscr'*/
#include <conio.h>
/* prototype of 'memmove'*/
#include <mem.h>
/* prototypes of 'printf', 'gets'*/
#include <stdio.h>
/* prototype of 'strncmpi'*/
#include <string.h>
/* prototypes of 'malloc', 'free'*/
#include <stdlib.h>

/* Since we'll need sqlcode and sqlmess_, we define them:*/
EXEC SQL INCLUDE SQLCA;

/* Since we'll need a SQLDA, we define it:*/
EXEC SQL INCLUDE SQLDA;

/* The above SQL statement 'include sqlda' will generate a C statement
similar to: '#include "sqlda_c.inc"'. Most database vendors provide
an include file which has both the structure declaration and the
allocation statement for an area named 'sqlda', with an arbitrary
maximum of sqlvar occurrences. If the maximum is insufficient for
your purposes, it is possible to either change the limit set by the
vendor, or define your own 'sqlda' using the structure shown previously.*/

/* The only host variable we need is 'command_string'. It will contain
the string that the user types in (accepted with the C 'gets'
function). We'll pass its value to the DBMS with 'exec sql describe
:command_string;' and 'exec sql execute :command_string;'.*/
```

# Listing 4.1 — continued

```
EXEC SQL BEGIN DECLARE SECTION;
     char command_string[255];
EXEC SQL END DECLARE SECTION;

/* Constants used for line drawing*/
#define BAR '|'              /* we use BAR to separate columns        */
#define UNDERLINE '-'        /* we use UNDERLINE to underline the header */

#define SCREENWIDTH 80

/* Procedure prototypes
There are only 2 procedures: one if the command is SELECT, one to fill*/
void doselect (void);
void display_sql_row (char *display_type);

void main ()
{
char *p;

clrscr();
/* Loop: get string from user, execute it, repeat till 'EXIT' seen. */
for (;;) {
/* Screen lines 1 to 3 are for "Command:" prompt and user input. We begin
by clearing them, since the last command might still be there.*/
     gotoxy(1,1); clreol();
     gotoxy(1,2); clreol();
     gotoxy(1,3); clreol();
     gotoxy(1,1); printf("Command:");
     gets(command_string); /* Get user input */
/* We must know in advance whether a command is SELECT or EXIT.*/
     for (p=command_string; *p==' '; ++p) ;     /* skip lead spaces */
     if (strnicmp(p,"EXIT",4)==0) break;        /* break if 'EXIT'  */
     if (strnicmp(p,"SELECT",6)==0) doselect(); /* do this if 'SELECT'*/
     else {
     EXEC SQL EXECUTE :command_string; }        /* do this if not    */
if (sqlcode>=0) {
     EXEC SQL COMMIT; }
     clrscr();
     gotoxy(1,LINE_5);
     printf("sqlcode=%d\n",sqlcode);
     printf("%s",sqlmess_); }
```

## Listing 4.1 — continued

```
/* We've exited the loop because the user typed the word 'EXIT'. */
clrscr(); }      /* and return to MS-DOS now.*/

/* Describe and Execute a command that contains a SELECT statement */
void doselect ()
{
int sql_column_number,sql_column_type,sql_column_width,j,k;
long int offset;
struct sqlvar *varptr;
int saved_sqlcode;
char saved_sqlmess_[255];
char far *malloc_area=0L;

/* If any SQL commands inside this procedure return an error, we'll
jump to f, which is a label towards the end of the procedure.*/
EXEC SQL WHENEVER SQLERROR GOTO f;
EXEC SQL DESCRIBE :command_string INTO :sqlda;   /* Fills sqlda/sqlvar */

/* The 'describe' gives us SQL column names, types, and sizes -- but not the
addresses. Setting up the addresses is the program's responsibility.
For this application, we've decided to use malloc() to create a
SINGLE area that's just large enough to fit the data that can be
returned. That means we'll loop through the sqlda twice -- the
first time we'll be adjusting the types and calculating the widths,
the second time we'll be adding the address of the malloc'd area to
the offsets we calculate.*/

offset=0;                               /* first loop through sqlda */
for (sql_column_number=0;
 sql_column_number<sqlda.sqld;++sql_column_number) {
    varptr=&sqlda.sqlvar[sql_column_number];
    sql_column_type=varptr->sqltype;
/* 448/449 is VARCHAR, 452/453 is CHAR */
if ((sql_column_type & 0xfffe)!=448 && (sql_column_type & 0xfffe)!=452) {

/* Next we force all non-character sqltypes to be 449 varying length
nullable character string (VARCHAR), and assume that our DBMS will
be able to automatically convert all numbers/dates/times/timestamps
to character strings when it passes to the host, and that none of
those types requires more than 20 bytes to store.*/
```

## Listing 4.1 — continued

```
    varptr->sqltype=449;            /* fiddle it to a varchar! */
    varptr->sqllen=20; }            /* fiddle the size to 20!  */
    sql_column_width=varptr->sqllen;
    offset+=sql_column_width+2;     /* calc next col offset    */
    offset+=sizeof(int); }          /* indicators are integers */
    if ((malloc_area=malloc(offset))==0L) goto f;
offset=0;
for (sql_column_number=0;           /* second loop through sqlda */

sql_column_number<sqlda.sqld;++sql_column_number) {
    varptr=&sqlda.sqlvar[sql_column_number];
    varptr->sqldata = malloc_area + offset;/* set data's address    */
    offset+=varptr->sqllen+2;
    varptr->sqlind = (int*)malloc_area+offset; /*set indicator's address*/
    offset+=sizeof(int); }

/* The setup of the sqlda descriptor area is now complete. From now on
the only thing that changes is the data stored *malloc_area --
because of the way that we set up the sqlda, each FETCH in the
forthcoming loop will be transferring data to designated addresses
within malloc_area.*/
gotoxy(1,LINE_LAST);          /* put prompt on the last line*/
printf("Type any key to fetch next row.");

/* On line 5, display column 'headings': field names are as gotten from 'describe'.*/
display_sql_row("heading");                    /* display heading */
for (k=0; k<SCREENWIDTH; ++k) putch(UNDERLINE);  /* underline heading*/

EXEC SQL DECLARE C CURSOR FOR :command_string;
/* Notice the "dynamic" form of the DECLARE here. This works out to
meaning "declare c cursor for <a SQL command written to the host
variable 'command_string'>;".*/

EXEC SQL OPEN C;/* Do selection         */
for (;;) {      /* i.e., "infinitely" */
    EXEC SQL FETCH C USING DESCRIPTOR :sqlda;   /* get 1 row*/
/* The FETCH here is also a "dynamic" variant. Instead of fetching
directly into variables as static SQL would, we fetch indirectly
into *malloc_area using the pointers supplied in sqlda.*/
```

## Listing 4.1 — continued

```
     if (sqlcode==100) break;          /* exit loop if no more rows*/
     display_sql_row("detail"); }       /* show row data on screen  */
gotoxy(1,LINE_LAST);
printf("Enter any key to end"); clreol();
getch();
f:
EXEC SQL WHENEVER SQLERROR CONTINUE;

/* When we return to the main loop, we want to display
sqlcode + sqlmess_. But the following 'close cursor' command will
change those variables. So we save them, close, and restore.
Technically, the 'close cursor' could be avoided because when
we exit the loop we do a COMMIT. COMMIT closes all open cursors.*/
saved_sqlcode=sqlcode; strcpy(saved_sqlmess_,sqlmess_);
EXEC SQL CLOSE C;
sqlcode=saved_sqlcode; strcpy(sqlmess_,saved_sqlmess_);
if (malloc_area!=0L) free(malloc_area); }

void display_sql_row (char *displaytype)
{
unsigned int    screen_column_width,line_number,max_line_number,k;
char linebuf[LINE_LAST][SCREENWIDTH]; /* store here before
                                        displaying rows*/
unsigned int    sql_column_number;
int   sql_column_width;
char far *sql_column_pointer;
char *screen_column_pointer;
struct          sqlvar *varptr;
static char     question_mark[]="?";
static int current_line,first_display_line;

/* Our method of dividing up the screen line into screen columns is
very simple: we'll just divide the screen width by the number of
SQL columns, which results in a situation where all screen columns
are the same size.*/
screen_column_width=SCREENWIDTH / sqlda.sqld;
setmem(linebuf,sizeof(linebuf),' ');    /* clear the buffer*/
max_line_number=0;
for (sql_column_number=0;
 sql_column_number<sqlda.sqld;++sql_column_number) {
     varptr=&sqlda.sqlvar[sql_column_number];
```

## Listing 4.1 — continued

```
/* There are three possible data locations:
1) if this is the heading, then the data is in varptr->sqlname,
2) if this is a detail row and the indicator value is less than 0,
   we'll use a question mark to signify it (it's conventional to
   use "?" for displaying NULLs),
3) if this is a detail row and the indicator value is greater than
   or equal to 0, the data is in what varptr->sqldata points to.*/
    if (strcmp(displaytype,"heading")==0) {
    sql_column_width=varptr->sqlname.length;
    sql_column_pointer=varptr->sqlname.data; }
    else {
    if (*(varptr->sqlind)<0) {
    sql_column_width=1;
    sql_column_pointer=question_mark; }    /* indicator NULL */
    else {
    sql_column_width=*((unsigned int *) varptr->sqldata);
    sql_column_pointer=varptr->sqldata+2; } }

/* We've got an array linebuf[LINE_LAST][SCREENWIDTH]  i.e., a 25x80 buffer.
Transfer from the SQL data location to the appropriate buffer location.*/
    for (line_number=0;;++line_number) {
    screen_column_pointer=
&linebuf[line_number][sql_column_number*screen_column_width];
    *(screen_column_pointer++)=BAR;  /* | to separate cols */
    if (sql_column_width<=0) break;
    for (k=1; k<screen_column_width && --sql_column_width>=0; ++k) {
    *(screen_column_pointer++)=*(sql_column_pointer++); } }
    if (line_number>max_line_number) max_line_number=line_number; }
```

# Listing 4.1 — continued

```c
/* We now have 'max_line_number' lines filled within 'linebuffer'.
First we scroll the window up so there's enough room to display.
Then we display.*/
if (strcmp(displaytype,"heading")==0) {
    for (current_line=LINE_LAST; current_line>=LINE_5; --current_line) {
    gotoxy(1,current_line);
    clreol(); }
    first_display_line=LINE_5+max_line_number+1; }
if (current_line+max_line_number>=LINE_LAST-1) {
    gotoxy(1,LINE_LAST);
    printf("Type any key to see next row.");
    getch();
    gotoxy(1,LINE_LAST);
    clreol();
    gotoxy(1,first_display_line);
    for (k=0; k<max_line_number; ++k) delline();
    gotoxy(1,current_line-1); }
else current_line+=max_line_number;
for (line_number=0; line_number<max_line_number; ++line_number) {
    for (k=0; k<SCREENWIDTH; ++k) putch(linebuf[line_number][k]); }
}


/* NOTES
1) For simplicity we have eliminated overflow testing. Both sqlda
   and command_string could overflow, and this should be tested for.
2) We didn't do a separate malloc() for every variable. In
   large-model Windows, the malloc() would probably be converted to
   GlobalAlloc(), and there's a limited number of GlobalAlloc()s
   that can be done with Windows 3.1. So the code calculates the
   total size, and subdivides that.
3) We didn't try to save a few bytes of data space by saying
   "if (the column is defined as NOT NULL) then (we won't require
   a word for the indicator integer)", on the theory that NOT NULL
   columns can't be NULL.  Actually, a 'select' with an outer join,
    e.g.,: "SELECT A.COL,B.COL FROM A LEFT JOIN B WHERE A.COL=B.COL"
   can return NULLs for B.COL. It doesn't matter that B.COL was
    defined as NOT NULL.
4) We use "sizeof(int)", not 2, because 32-bit code is becoming
   increasingly common these days. Symantec C++ users should
   replace this with __INTSIZE.*/
```

# *ODBC*

Microsoft's "Open Database Connectivity" (ODBC) is a new and different way to interface a C host program and an SQL engine. While embedded SQL is precompiled into an API, ODBC is one level lower: it is an API. Figures 5.1 and 5.2 show the differing philosophies of embedded SQL and ODBC. Embedded SQL's current advantage is a fact: embedded SQL source code looks similar regardless of vendor or platform. ODBC's near-future advantage is a promise: ODBC binary-level object code is plug-and-playable from any application on a Windows platform.

ODBC is "OPEN" (Microsoft made the specification but anyone can build for it) "DATABASE" (whatever that means; neither Microsoft's document or the ANSI SQL standard define just what a database is supposed to be) "CONNECTIVITY" (the big idea is that compliant applications can call compliant drivers under Windows).

The specification is not vague. There is a thick document (Microsoft's Open Database Connectivity Software Development Kit, v1.0, 1992) which sets out the call names and parameter types, the range of allowed values, the possible error returns, and the accompanying actions. (v2.0 of the Software Development Kit is expected in mid-1994.)

Notice that compliance with ODBC is not the same as compliance with SQL, because ODBC is for the packaging and SQL is for the contents.

For example, consider this ODBC call:

```
retcode=SQLExecDirect(hstmt,"INSERT INTO TABLE1 VALUES (1)", SQL_NTS);
```

The ODBC specification tells us what *SQLExecDirect* is: it's a function that returns an integer. All calls are far, and all parameters are passed last-to-first as in the Pascal model. For this specific function, there are three parameters: a handle to a statement (which we'll get to later), a null-terminated string containing a valid SQL statement, and a size (*SQL_NTS* is a constant for "null-terminated string").

Our metaphor will be that ODBC's job is the specification of a missile. The warhead is the SQL statement:

```
insert into table1 values (1)
```

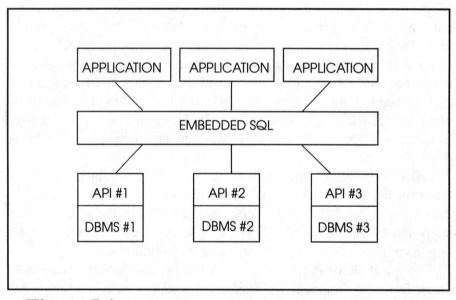

**Figure 5.1**  *Embedded SQL invokes the DBMS through a vendor-specific API (Application Programming Interface). Since the API designer knows what's in his own DBMS, he can build a more efficient interface. But because each DBMS requires a different API, programs are portable at the embedded SQL level (source code level) only.*

The ODBC Software Development Kit has an appendix in which the rules of SQL grammar are set out formally but tersely. The appendix says the grammar is based on ANSI SQL. In fact there are some differences. (For instance, SQL 92 says that outer joins can be *LEFT* or *RIGHT* or *FULL*, but the ODBC appendix only mentions *LEFT* outer joins.) But the differences are primarily in the advanced stuff. So, while there is such a thing as "ODBC SQL," it's not in competition with the real standard. Microsoft leaves the SQL formalities to the ANSI committee in charge of the SQL standard, and variations between vendors' SQL implementations will not seriously affect their ability to comply with the ODBC API itself.

In our missile metaphor, the guy with the finger on the firing button is you, the application programmer. By following both the ODBC rules and the ANSI rules, you control a considerable arsenal.

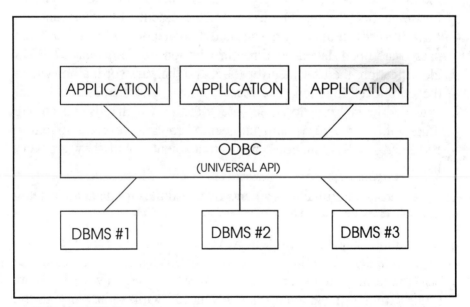

**Figure 5.2**  *The ODBC interface is compatible with any participating DBMS. Applications are portable at the binary level, but the API is not sensitive to vendor-specific nuances. The programmer can invoke the API directly, thus skipping a step, but the "deeper level" ODBC code is sometimes harder to read, and comes without the labor-saving niceties of a precompiler.*

# Compliance Levels

The Microsoft ODBC document states what "ODBC compliant" means:

APIs which do exactly what this specification says are ODBC-compliant.

There does not appear to be a similar specification about what "ODBC compatible" means. Two "ODBC compatible" packages may break some of the specification's rules (therefore they're not "compliant"), but work together anyway.

There are three levels of API compliance:

☐ Core-level functions are the fundamental functions necessary for any serious applications. The *SQLExecDirect* function, which we saw above, is a core function; so are the functions for setting up the environment, connecting to the database, and checking for errors.

☐ Extended-level-1 functions provide additional information and allow for some fine tuning. For example, the extended-level-1 function *SQLDriverConnect* allows driver-specific connection information to be passed at "open database" time (in addition to the database/DBMS identification, the user identification, and the password, all of which the core-level function, *SQLConnect*, allows you to pass.) Another extended-level-1 function is *SQLGetStmtOption*, which tells you, among other things, the maximum number of rows a *select* can return. Extended-level-1 functions aren't fundamental, but they are very handy.

☐ Extended-level-2 functions are mostly substitutes for database catalog queries.

In addition to the three levels of API compliance, there are three levels of SQL compliance: minimum (very low, for instance, the only data type is *CHAR*), intermediate (where most serious SQL vendors will be, except for fairly minor deviations), and advanced (with some very useful extensions).

# ODBC Functions: The Basics

All ODBC functions have common features:

☐ Their names always begin with the letters "SQL."

☐ The calls are far.

Parameters are passed by value or by (far) address. There can be from one to 12 parameters, depending on the call. When a function has more than one parameter, the order of parameter-passing is from first to last. This is the Pascal calling convention and is the reverse of the way that C normally passes parameters, but it conforms to the way parameters are usually passed using the Windows SDK.

When a string parameter is passed, it is usually accompanied by a *long int* "size of string" parameter, which in C will often be equal to *SQL_NTS* (see below), which equals –3 (minus 3) and means "null-terminated string."

All functions return an integer value. This value will be one of:

☐ 0 = *SQL_SUCCESS* (all went well);

☐ -1 = *SQL_ERROR* (all did not go well; for further information you'll have to call the *SQLError* function);

☐ +100 = *SQL_NOTFOUND* (there are no more rows to *fetch*); or

☐ +1 = *SQL_SUCCESS_WITH_INFO* (all went well, but there's a warning or informative message; again you'll have to call *SQLError* for further information).

Vendors can, and probably should, supply an *include* file with the declarations and function prototypes that make enforcement of the rules easy for C programmers. Listing 5.1 shows part of the *include* file *sql.h*, which comes with Microsoft's kit for the ODBC core functions.

# Core Functions: The Basics

The ODBC core functions aren't uniquely ODBCish. The basic spec was devised by a committee of SQL vendors called the SQL Access Group ("SAG" for short), and programs which are restricted to the ODBC core functions could just as well be called "SAG compliant," or even "IDAPI compliant" (IDAPI is an API specification promoted by some major Microsoft competitors, including Borland International).

The core functions can be grouped into five categories:

☐ The *handshaking functions* allow the program to establish a connection and to shut the connection down.

☐ The *action functions* allow the program to prepare and execute an SQL statement, to cancel a statement (*rollback*), or to end a transaction (*commit*).

☐ The *error-or-warning-information functions* allow the program to find out what went wrong with any of the other functions, and to find out how many rows were affected by some of the other functions.

☐ The *host variable functions* allow the program to transfer data between SQL and C.

☐ The *select-support functions* allow the program to process the results of a *select*.

This list of function groups is our "view from a height." Now we descend a bit and make a pass over the same ground so that we can make out the actual structures. Keep in mind in the next few pages that we are still not on the ground, though. The descriptions are correct as far as they go, but if we listed all the exceptions and special circumstances, we'd

## Listing 5.1

```
/* generally useful constants */
#define SQL_NTS -3                     /*NTS=Null Terminated String */
#define SQL_SQLSTATE_SIZE 5            /*size of SQLSTATE           */
#define SQL_MAX_MESSAGE_LENGTH 512     /*message buffer size        */
#define SQL_MAX_DSN_LENGTH 32          /*maximum datasourcename size*/

/* RETCODEs */
#define SQL_ERROR            -1
#define SQL_INVALID_HANDLE   -2
#define SQL_NEED_DATA        99
#define SQL_NO_DATA_FOUND    100
```

# Listing 5.1 — continued

```c
#define SQL_SUCCESS          0
#define SQL_SUCCESS_WITH_INFO     1

/* SQL portable types for C */
typedef unsigned char      UCHAR;
typedef signed char        SCHAR;
typedef long int           SDWORD;
typedef short int          SWORD;
typedef unsigned long int  UDWORD;
typedef unsigned short int UWORD;
typedef double             SDOUBLE;
typedef long double        LDOUBLE;
typedef float              SFLOAT;
typedef void FAR *         PTR;
typedef void FAR *         HENV;
typedef void FAR *         HDBC;
typedef void FAR *         HSTMT;
typedef int                RETCODE;

/* Core Function Prototypes */
RETCODE SQL_API SQLAllocConnect(
     HENV        henv,
     HDBC FAR  * phdbc);

RETCODE SQL_API SQLAllocEnv(
     HENV FAR  * phenv);


RETCODE SQL_API SQLAllocStmt(
     HDBC         hdbc,
     HSTMT FAR  * phstmt);

RETCODE SQL_API SQLBindCol(
     HSTMT        hstmt,
     UWORD        icol,
     SWORD        fCType,
     PTR          rgbValue,
     SDWORD       cbValueMax,
     SDWORD FAR * pcbValue);
```

have to devote several pages to each function. At this still-introductory stage, we have pruned out the superfluities.

*Note: Descriptive pseudo-names (in bullets) are shown within double quote marks to distinquish them from actual commands.*

# Core Handshaking Functions

The two types of handshaking functions are those that establish a connection:

☐ "Allocate Environment area"

☐ "Allocate Connection area"

☐ "Connect to database"

☐ "Allocate Statement area"

and those that shut down a connection:

☐ "Free Statement area"

☐ "Disconnect from database"

☐ "Free Connection area"

☐ "Free Environment area"

Where can a DBMS store its own program-data variables?

It can store some data on the stack, but some data — the handle of an open file, for example — is semi-permanent and can't be erased between function calls.

It can store everything in a static reserved data segment like *DGROUP*, but under Windows a DLL isn't re-entrant if it has a static data segment with initialized or semi-permanent variables.

Once upon a time, The Primeval Programmer saw these two design constraints — "some data must be preserved across calls and the library is preferably re-entrant" — and responded: "In that case, I have to dynamically allocate space when I initialize, which I'll free when I exit. I can't even store the address of this space, but the calling program can — so I'll return an address or handle to the calling program when I do my allocation and expect the calling program to pass that to me as a parameter of every call."

If you believe this plausible fable, you will have no trouble understanding why the first ODBC function you'll use is "Allocate Environment":

```
retcode=SQLAllocEnv(&henv);
```

where *&henv* is a pointer to an "environment handle."

It's the ODBC driver that needs an environment — the application doesn't use it, and doesn't have to know what's in it. The environment's only job is store the returned handle.

A similar story line applies for "Allocate Connection":

```
retcode=SQLAllocConnect(henv,&hdbc);
```

The application passes the environment handle that it got with *SQLAllocEnv*, and gets back a "connection handle." Again, the application's only job is to store the returned handle.

Now we can "Connect to a data source":

```
retcode=SQLConnect(hdbc,datasource_name,datasource_name_size,
    user_identifier,user_identifier_size,authentication_string,
    authentication_string_size);
```

This time you have to provide the application with some specific information; for example, "what's a data source?" The following definition isn't the official one (which is too murky), it's just the most probable one in the current real world: "The data source is the DBMS (or SQL engine) called by the ODBC driver, plus the linkage between the driver and the SQL engine, e.g., a network protocol, plus the database itself." Thus, *datasource_name* will change whenever your application switches to another DBMS product.

But whatever an application program does, there's a one-to-one connection between it and the database it ultimately wants to access; so, by oversimplifying vastly, we say that *SQLConnect* is the way we "open the database," since it supplies the necessary linkage information. The *user_identifier* would be somebody's name, or somebody's title, and the *authentication_string* would be a password.

Now we can "Allocate a Statement Handle":

```
retcode=SQLAllocStmt(hdbc,&hstmt);
```

So now we have one environment handle, one connection handle, and one statement handle. We could, in fact, have two connection handles so an application can connect to two databases, or two statement handles so an application can have two cursors open at once or even run processes asynchronously. All simple programs, though, will just do *SQLAllocEnv + SQLAllocConnect + SQLConnect + SQLAllocStmt* as shown above, and once they're done, "initialization" is complete.

The shutting down process is taken care of by four functions that are exactly the reverse of the four initialization functions and would appear in reverse order, thus:

```
retcode=SQLFreeStmt(hstmt,SQL_DROP);
retcode=SQLDisconnect(hdbc);
retcode=SQLFreeConnect(hdbc);
retcode=SQLFreeEnv(henv);
```

Normally, of course, between the initialization and the shutting down, we would actually do something. That is, we would call one or more action functions.

## *Core Action Functions*

The core action functions are:

☐ "Prepare an SQL statement"

☐ "Execute an already-prepared SQL statement"

☐ "Execute an SQL statement directly" (both prepare and execute it)

☐ "Cancel an SQL statement" (*rollback*)

☐ "End a transaction" (*commit*)

At the beginning of this chapter, we described *SQLExecDirect* as a warhead function. All the explosive punch in ODBC is packed in the SQL, and the way we do an SQL string's thing is by "Executing Directly an SQL String":

```
retcode=SQLExecDirect(hstmt,sql_string,size_of_sql_string);
```

where *sql_string* could be, for example, any of the following:

```
insert into table1 values (1)

alter table table1 add column2 char(100)

update table1 set column2= 'a' || 'b'

drop table table1
```

and so on.

The only DBMS activities you can't instigate with *SQLExecDirect* are connecting (as we saw earlier, there's an *SQLConnect* call for that), fetching rows (as we'll see later, there's an *SQLFetch* call for that), *commit*, and *rollback*.

*commit* and *rollback* require a made-for-the-purpose ODBC call:

```
retcode=SQLTransact(henv,hdbc,SQL_COMMIT);
```

and

```
retcode=SQLTransact(henv,hdbc,SQL_ROLLBACK);
```

Presumably, we can't:

```
SQLExecDirect(hstmt,"COMMIT",sizeof ("COMMIT"));
```

because you don't just *commit* one statement. You commit *all* of the statements that have been done since the last *commit* or *rollback* for the whole connection, or perhaps the whole environment. So we want a call that passes the connection handle (*hdbc*) or the environment handle (*henv*), not the statement handle (*hstmt*). (That's the best excuse we can think of anyway. Actually, we think *SQLTransact* is function-call bloat.)

ODBC has another characteristic important to *commit* and *rollback* functions: the default is "autocommit" for every SQL statement. The default can be overridden with an extended-level-1 function call; however, one gets the impression that ODBC's designers didn't want to make transaction control too easy.

Now, let's take a moment to shed some pity for the overloaded *SQLExecDirect* function. It's been saddled with multiple duties — it has to parse and bind the SQL statement, and then it has to execute it. In other words, it's the equivalent of embedded dynamic SQL's

```
exec sql execute immediate :string;
```

which means there's a performance hit, if you remember your Chapter 4. So instead of doing everything in one *SQLExecDirect* call, one can do the parsing/binding in an *SQLPrepare* call, and then do the execution alone in an *SQLExecute* call, viz.:

```
retcode=SQLPrepare(hstmt,sql_string,size_of_sql_string);
retcode=SQLExecute(hstmt);
```

Thus, in the following, the code in Column A is equivalent to that in Column B:

```
Column A                          Column B

strcpy(s,"DELETE FROM T");        strcpy(s,"DELETE FROM T");
s_size=strlen(s)+1;               s_size=strlen(s)+1;
SQLPrepare(hstmt,s,s_size);       for (i=0; i<1000; ++i) {
for (i=0; i<1000; ++i) {          SQLExecDirect(hstmt,s,s_size);
SQLExecute(hstmt);                }
}
```

but Column A's code is better because some action is removed from the loop.

We couldn't do a "hello world" program till now, because almost all the handshaking and action functions are needed in even the simplest program. But it is now possible:

```
#include "sql.h"
HENV henv;
HDBC hdbc;
HSTMT hstmt;
void main ()
{
SQLAllocEnv(&henv);
SQLAllocConnect(henv,&hdbc);
SQLConnect(hdbc,"database",SQL_NTS,"user",SQL_NTS,"password",SQL_NTS);
SQLAllocStmt(hdbc,&hstmt);

SQLExecDirect(hstmt,"insert into table1 values ('Hello world')",
              SQL_NTS);
SQLTransact(henv,hdbc,SQL_COMMIT); /* not strictly necessary here */
SQLFreeStmt(hstmt,SQL_DROP);
SQLDisconnect(hdbc);
SQLFreeConnect(hdbc);
SQLFreeEnv(henv);
}
```

The above code will insert the string *Hello world* into the lone column of table *table1* in database *database*.

# Core Error-and-Warning-Information Functions

It's possible to write a program without testing for errors — we just did. But the program could have failed anywhere along the line. For instance, we know that the SQL engine will almost certainly try to allocate some RAM space for itself when an *SQLAlloc()* function calls it, so what if the Windows SDK's *GlobalAlloc* function, or whatever the engine is using, returns a "no space" error?

An application's first line of defense is:

```
if (return_code_from_ODBC_function_call==SQL_ERROR) {
/* possibly: find out more about the error condition,
   do something about the error condition, or display, or abort */
}
```

Recall that the error return code from an ODBC function call has only five possible states: *SQL_ERROR*, *SQL_SUCCESS*, *SQL_SUCCESS_WITH_INFO*, *SQL_NOTFOUND*, and *SQL_INVALID_HANDLE*.

In information theory terms, this is less than three bits of information. Often one needs more, and often one can get more, with:

```
retcode=SQLError(henv,hdbc,hstmt,sqlstate_string,&native_error,
    error_message_string,maximum_size_of_error_message_string,
    &actual_size_of_error_message_string_that_could_have_been_returned);
```

Additionally, remember that in embedded SQL, there are some returned variables which are "always there"; for instance, *sqlcode* (the integer containing an error status code) or *SQLSTATE* (a string used for the same purpose) are set automatically by the SQL engine after executing every embedded SQL statement. In ODBC, it's different. *SQLError* must be explicitly called.

ODBC's *native_error* is just *sqlcode* with a different name (and maybe a different size: *native_error* is a 32-bit integer). And the *error_message_string* we get with *SQLError* is the equivalent of the error message we got in embedded SQL.

*SQLSTATE*, as we said in Chapter 3, is the new, standardized way of expressing status information in SQL 92 as a five-character, null-terminated string.

While *sqlcode* (or, if you prefer the ODBC term, *native_error*) was a fine and meaningful integer, nobody could agree whether *-321* meant "internal error; table handle not open" (as in Oracle) or "invalid *CONFIG.XDB*" (as in XDB). The *SQLSTATE* string *22012*, on the other hand, means "division by zero" to everybody who pays attention to SQL 92.

So if you're trying to write a generalized program, you should prefer the *SQLSTATE* check shown below in Column A. If, however, your application is tied to a particular SQL engine, the code in Column B is slightly more efficient:

| Column A | Column B |
|---|---|
| `if (strcmp(SQLSTATE,"22012") == 0) {`<br>`printf("division by 0!\n"); }` | `if (sqlcode == -802) {`<br>`printf("division by 0!\n"); }` |

You can use the following code to add a generalized error test after the *SQLExecDirect* example statement:

```
char SQLSTATE[6];
long int sqlcode;
char message[SQL_MAX_MESSAGE_LENGTH+1];      /* i.e., 512+1 */
int actual_message_length;
...
SQLExecDirect(hstmt,"insert into table1 values (1)",SQL_NTS);
if (retcode==SQL_ERROR) {
    printf("Error after call to SQLExecDirect function!\n");
    SQLError(0,0,hstmt,SQLSTATE,&sqlcode,message,
        SQL_MAX_MESSAGE_LENGTH,&actual_message_length);
    printf("Sqlstate=%s.\n",SQLSTATE);
    printf("Native error code=%ld.\n",sqlcode);
    printf("Message=%s.\n",message);
    if (actual_message_length>SQL_MAX_MESSAGE_LENGTH) {
        printf("[Message was truncated]\n"); }
    exit(1); }
```

If one wanted to get all the warning information, one could have a similar routine for the case *if(retcode==SQL_SUCCESS_WITH_INFO )* .... There is no ODBC equivalent to the *exec sql whenever* directives we saw with embedded SQL, so one has to add such a routine, or a call to it, after every statement that might be realistically expected to have a problem. We have left *SQLError* out of our examples to avoid clutter, but you should assume it's always there.

Besides *SQLError*, there's another ODBC function that gives us a bit of information about what a previous ODBC function call accomplished:

```
retcode=SQLRowCount(hstmt,&pcrow);
```

Microsoft's document says, "*SQLRowCount* returns the number of rows affected by an *update*, *insert*, or *delete* statement ... for other requests, the driver may define the value of *pcrow*." But the word "affected" is not defined, and Microsoft's own ODBC core validation test will reject drivers that return anything other than 0 (zero) for "other requests." So avoid *SQLRowCount* unless you're working with a particular ODBC driver and you know what it's going to do.

# *Core Host Variable Functions*

Let's re-introduce the host variable passing we did with embedded SQL:

```
exec sql begin declare section;
    long int hostvariable;
    int indicator;
exec sql end declare section;
...
exec sql insert into t values (:hostvariable :indicator);
```

With ODBC, our objective is no different. We still want to pass the contents of the host variable *hostvariable* to the SQL engine. And the SQL engine still needs to know more about *hostvariable* than just its address, because not all passes to the database are of the same data type or size.

In the example above, the precompiler has an easy time getting the information because it reads the source code and thus sees the actual *int hostvariable* declaration. Now though, we're dealing with an API, so there *is* no source code. We therefore have to pass a description of the parameter(s) to an action call. That's what the *SQLSetParam* function call is for. The program uses *SQLSetParam* to tell the SQL engine, in advance, for an SQL statement it's about to execute, what a single parameter's (i.e., host variable's) type, size and address are. Specifically, the program passes the information in this order: the ordinal (base 1) number of the parameter, the C type, the SQL type, the precision, the scale, the address, and the "length" (sort of). One calls *SQLSetParam* as many times as the SQL statement has *?* placeholders for host variables (not indicators).

For example, we could replace the embedded-SQL snippet above with this:

```
long int hostvariable;
long int indicator;
...
SQLSetParam(hstmt,1,SQL_C_LONG,SQL_INTEGER,0,0,
    &hostvariable,&indicator);
ExecSqlDirect(hstmt,"insert into t values (?)",SQL_NTS);
```

In the *SQLSetParam* call shown above, the parameters represent the following:

a) The *1* means that "this is the *SQLSetParam* call for the first parameter in the following SQL statement." (Looking down we see that there is only one question mark, so only one *SQLSetParam* call is required.)

b) The *SQL_C_LONG* means "this is a 32-bit integer in C," which corresponds with *SQL_INTEGER*, meaning "this is a 32-bit integer in SQL."

c) The next two parameters (*0* and *0*) are the precision and scale, which we don't care about for integers, so we say *0* twice.

d) *&hostvariable* is the address of the host variable itself.

e) The parameter *indicator* isn't quite the same as embedded SQL's indicator variable, but we do set it to *-1* if we're passing *NULL*. (Actually our copy of the Microsoft document says this indicator is "ignored for numeric data types," but that's so silly we've assumed it's a mistake in our copy.)

Voila. With *SQLSetParam*, we can pass host variables forth.

Notice that we didn't say "back and forth." This is because ODBC has a different function call if we're going the other way! For the one and only time that we're taking data from SQL and putting it in C host variables, which is to say when we're handling the list of variables in the *into* clause of a *select* statement, we have to use *SQLBindCol* instead. We're passing by address in either case, and the information we have to pass about address and size and type isn't much different — the only distinction is that data's going in the opposite direction. The reversed *SQLSetParam* function looks like this:

```
retcode=SQLBindCol(hstmt,column_number,c_type,
     &address,max_length,&indicator);
```

In practice, you will find *SQLBindCol* just before a *fetch* loop.

## *Core Select-Support Functions*

The core *select*-support functions are:

☐ "Get the number of result columns"

☐ "Get the name of the cursor"

☐ "Set the name of the cursor"

☐ "Fetch a row"

☐ "Describe one column"

☐ "Get the attributes of a column"

☐ "Cancel a cursor" (There's no specific "close cursor" function.)

In ODBC (unlike in embedded dynamic SQL) a *select* statement gets passed just like other SQL statements:

```
retcode=SQLExecDirect(hstmt,
    "SELECT S1 INTO ? FROM TABLE1",SQL_NTS);
```

But, once again, we encounter the special problems that dynamic *select* statements bring in their train. The easy situation — when we know in advance how many host variables there are and what their types are — can be handled by introducing a row-fetching loop. But the loop differs from the embedded static SQL *fetch* loop we saw in Chapter 3:

```
/* static embedded-SQL SELECT */
exec sql begin declare section;
    char hostvariable[13];
exec sql end declare section;
...
exec sql declare FROM_TAB1 select s1 from table1;
exec sql open FROM_TAB1;
for (;;) {
    exec sql fetch FROM_TAB1 into :hostvariable;
    if (sqlcode==100) break;
    printf("the value of s1 is: %s.\n",hostvariable); }
exec sql close FROM_TAB1;
```

Instead, it looks like this:

```
/* ODBC equivalent */
char hostvariable[13];
...
SQLExecDirect(hstmt,"select s1 into ? from table1",SQL_NTS);
SQLBindCol(hstmt,1,SQL_C_CHAR,SQL_CHAR,hostvariable,12,NULL);
for (;;) {
    retcode=SQLFetch(hstmt);
    if (retcode==100) break;
    printf("the value of s1 is: %s.\n",hostvariable); }
SQLFreeStmt(hstmt,SQL_CLOSE);
```

In the above example, *SQLBindCol* associates the C host variable, *hostvariable*, with the parameter marker *?* in our *select*. We only need to do the association once, so we placed *SQLBindCol* outside the *SQLFetch* loop. Contrast that with embedded SQL where you have to do the "binding" every time you *fetch* a row.

Of course, this means that you can't let the address of *hostvariable* change between the time you call *SQLBindCol* and the time you call *SQLFetch*, but in C that's a safe assumption provided you don't do anything like call the stupid procedure in Figure 5.3 twice.

The rest of the ODBC fetch loop is straightforward. We check if *SQLFetch* returns *SQL_NOTFOUND* (i.e., 100, no need to call *SQLError* for this),

```
void stupid_procedure()
{
static int first_time_in_flag=TRUE;
char hostvariable[13];              /* automatics are on the stack        */
....
if (first_time_in_flag) {
    SQLBindCol(hstmt,1,SQL_C_CHAR,SQL_CHAR,hostvariable,12,NULL);
    first_time_in_flag=FALSE; }
if (SQLFetch(hstmt)==100) {          /* assume hostvariable hasn't moved */
    SQLFreeStmt(hstmt,SQL_CLOSE); }
else {
    printf("the value of s1 is: %s.\n",hostvariable); }
}
```

**Figure 5.3**   *Don't use this procedure.* hostvariable *is on the stack so its address can change.*

and if it doesn't, we display the result. If it does return 100, we clean up with *SQLFreeStmt(hstmt,SQL_CLOSE)*.

The last time we saw the *SQLFreeStmt* function call was when we were actually freeing the statement with *SQLFreeStmt(hstmt,SQL_DROP)*, but on this occasion we're leaving the statement handle in existence. All we do with the *SQL_CLOSE* option is close the cursor.

There is another core function that has the same effect as *SQLFreeStmt(hstmt,SQL_CLOSE)*, namely:

```
SQLCancel(hstmt);
```

In a multi-threaded environment, we could also use *SQLCancel* to abort a statement which we've launched but which hasn't returned yet.

By the way, it's OK to use words like "closing the cursor" even though our ODBC example never used a cursor. In ODBC, if we had two selections going at once, we'd just set up two statement handles; that is, we'd call *SQLAllocStmt* for each one. The concept of cursorhood still exists though. In fact, there are two function calls which specifically can get and set the cursor name:

```
retcode = SQLGetCursorName(hstmt,cursor_name,max_cursor_name_size,
    actual_cursor_name_size);
retcode = SQLSetCursorName(hstmt,cursor_name,cursor_name_size);
```

These are core functions, but their utility is pretty limited. The only time an ODBC programmer needs to care about a cursor name is when the SQL statement to be executed is either *update ... where current of <cursor>* or *delete ... where current of <cursor>*. Not stuff you do on day one.

Now we are ready for our final assault on SQL's summit: dynamic *select*. ODBC provides no direct equivalent of embedded SQL's *exec sql describe...*, but it does have two "helper functions" that give us the information we want. Both of these functions would be called if and only if we've just called *SQLExecDirect* (or *SQLPrepare*) with a *select* statement.

The first of these two functions tells us how many columns got selected:

```
retcode = SQLNumResultCols(hstmt,&pccol);
```

Getting *pccol* from *SQLNumResultCols* is the equivalent of getting *sqlda.sqld* from *exec sql describe* ....

The other function gets a column description:

```
retcode = SQLDescribeCol(hstmt,column_number,column_name,
    max_column_name_size,&actual_column_name_size,
    &sqltype,&precision,&scale,&nullable);
```

We have to call *SQLDescribeCol* once for each column — that is, we have to call it *pccol* times. The *column_number* parameter is the base-1 ordinal number of the column.

Following *column_number* is a typical trio: the address of the string variable that will receive the column-name, the maximum size of this string, and the actual size of the name. (You saw this address+max+actual trio when we discussed *SQLError*; ODBC likes to receive strings this way.)

The type, precision, scale, and nullability have exact equivalents in embedded SQL (although, unfortunately, the values are not the same), so the same general observations we made in Chapter 4 apply here, too, and we won't repeat them. The challenge our client posed in that chapter — how to execute anything the user types in — could be met in ODBC using the code in Listing 5.2.

There is one last core level ODBC function to mention: *SQLColAttributes*. Since there's nothing you can do with *SQLColAttributes* that you can't already do with *SQLDescribeCol*, there's no need to do more than mention it. So this is the end of the core-function descriptions.

## Listing 5.2

```
/* This 'subproc' procedure is a rough replacement for the complete
dynamic SQL example shown at the end of Chapter 4. Some crude assumptions
are made (for instance, that all columns are CHAR, and that there is no
need to free what we malloc). Mainly, we are trying to illustrate the
parallels between embedded SQL's "sqlda" (SQL dynamic area) and the ODBC
way by forcing the results of ODBC calls into a sqlda, as if we'd
described it. */
```

# Listing 5.2 — continued

```c
void subproc ()
{
char string[255];
char *p;
int columns,i;
/* include 'sqlda' descriptor as illustrated in previous chapter */
int   namesize=18;
int   actual_namesize;

printf("Type in any SQL string\n");      /* prompt               */
gets(string);                            /* get user's command   */
p=string;
while (isspace(*p)) ++p;                  /* skip lead spaces     */
retcode=SQLExecDirect(hstmt,p,SQL_NTS);
if (strnicmp(p,"SELECT",6)!=0) {          /* is it SELECT?        */
    SQLTransact(henv,hdbc,SQL_COMMIT); }/* no, so it's simple     */
else {
    SQLNumResultCols(hstmt,&columns);    /* get: how many columns */
    sqlda=malloc(columns*sizeof(struct sqlda));
    for (i=0; i<columns; ++i) {           /* loop for each column: */
        varptr=&sqlda[i];
a:  varptr->colname[i]=malloc(namesize);
    SQLDescribeCol(hstmt,i+1,             /* get info on 1 column  */
    varptr->colname,namesize,&actual_namesize,
    varptr->sqltype,
    varptr->sqllen,
    NULL,
    NULL);
    if (actual_namesize>namesize) {       /* if (name is too small): */
        free(colname[i]);                 /* release it,             */
        namesize=actual_namesize;         /* make it bigger,         */
        goto a; }                         /*  and retry.             */
    varptr->sqldata=(UCHAR *) malloc(varptr-sqllen);
    varptr->sqlind =(SWORD *) malloc(sizeof(int));
    SQLBindCol(hstmt,i+1,
    varptr->coltype,varptr->sqldata,varptr->sqllen,varptr->sqlind); }
for (;;) {                                /* loop for each row:    */
    if (SQLFetch(hstmt)==100) break;      /* get row, stop if end  */
    for (i=1;i<columns; ++i) {            /* loop for each column: */
        printf("(%s): %s.\n",varptr->sqldata); } } }
```

# A Quick Look at Some Non-Core Functions

We won't cover the non-core functions in detail as we did the core ones. There are a few functions, though, which are so fundamental that you might expect to find them even if the ODBC driver is officially just "core level."

*SQLGetInfo* is an extended-level-1 function which (among other things) returns "the level of ODBC (API) conformance: 0 = none, 1 = extended-level-1 supported, 2 = extended-level-2 supported." But, how do you ask the driver if it supports extended-level-1, if the fact that it's only core level means it doesn't have to support *SQLGetInfo*? So a sensible driver supplier supports it anyway.

*SQLExtendedFetch* is an extended-level-2 upgrade of *SQLFetch*, which lets us specify (among other things) the type of *fetch*, i.e., "fetch next," "fetch previous," "fetch last," etc. In other words, scroll cursors are extended-level-2. Most drivers today support scroll cursors, and most buyers demand them.

The following "catalog" functions are extended-level-2 functions that return information about the structure of the data in a database:

☐ *SQLColumnPrivileges* returns a list of columns and the privileges granted on them.

☐ *SQLColumns* returns a list of the names of the columns defined for a specified table.

☐ *SQLForeignKeys* returns a list of the names of the columns that comprise foreign keys for a specified table.

☐ *SQLPrimaryKeys* returns a list of the names of the columns that make up a specified table's primary key.

☐ *SQLSpecialColumns* returns information about the optimal set of columns that uniquely identify a row of data in a table, or the columns that are automatically updated when any value in the row is updated.

☐ *SQLStatistics* returns a list of statistics about a single table and its indexes.

☐ *SQLTablePrivileges* returns a list of the privileges granted on one or more tables.

☐ *SQLTables* returns a list of all the tables stored in a specified data source.

Each of these functions returns the information it provides as a result set. An application program retrieves the results by calling *SQLBindCol* and *SQLFetch*, just as with a regular query.

## *Choosing Among Compliance Levels*

Because there are 3 x 3 = 9 possible combinations of ODBC compliance when we consider both the API and the SQL grammar, an application which requires ODBC compatibility won't necessarily plug into an SQL engine that's simply billed as "ODBC compatible." So anyone concerned about connectivity hassles will want to pick the least-common-denominator on the demand side and the highest possible on the supply side. That is, one would write one's programs using only core API functions (and buy utility programs which don't require advanced SQL grammar) but require compliance with "extended-level-2 ODBC API" and "advanced SQL grammar" when selecting an ODBC driver.

Unfortunately, many ODBC-using programs simply have to use at least some non-core functionality. For instance, when Pioneer Software was asked about their Q+E package, they said it needed drivers which had "all of core, most of extended-level-1, and a few things in extended-level-2." We know of an SQL DBMS vendor that claims its driver complies with "the core level ODBC API, plus all the really important extended-level-1 and -2 functions," but as you might have guessed, this DBMS won't connect to Q+E.

Here's one reason why both application and DBMS will have to go beyond the core. All row fetching is sequential in core and extended-level-1; that is, the ODBC core level function *SQLFetch* can only get the "next" row. To fetch the previous, the first, the last, or the nth row, in other words to have the functional equivalent of what embedded SQL's scroll cursors provide, you need an ODBC function, *SQLExtendedFetch*, which is defined as extended-level-2. Most SQL implementations have no trouble with scroll cursors even if they can't handle most of the other extended-level-2 functionality — to them, scrolling is part of the "core."

This just illustrates that the distinctions between the ODBC levels are somewhat arbitrary.

With all the attention on levels of compliance, it is easy to conclude that a lack of functions implies a lack of functionality, but this isn't always the case. For instance, suppose you are writing an application that requires getting a list of all the tables in the database. The extended-level-2 function *SQLTables* provides this information, but if your ODBC driver doesn't support *SQLTables*, you can still get the same information by querying the database catalog directly — for example (if you have an IBM DB2-compatible SQL engine) with the statement:

```
select name from systables;
```

If the functionality is there, the absence of a particular ODBC function is not a disqualifier for the product. It just represents an added cost — you can always write your own implementation of the function.

The ODBC-supplying programs that promise everything will demand a lot too. We don't mean just that they're hideously expensive, but that they require lots of RAM and, according to some informal tests we've heard about, perform only as well as some of the cheap options that just supply the basics.

Before you buy then, we recommend that you do some research beyond just finding out what levels of ODBC conformance are supplied and demanded. Try to find out precisely what functions you really need. Figure out what weighting to give to the functions at the higher levels. Our advice is to buy your application and your DBMS at the same time and insist on 30-day money-back guarantees for both; that way you'll have just enough time to find out whether they really work together using the only safe method: try it yourself.

# Converting From ODBC to Embedded SQL

Compare a simple embedded SQL program to a simple ODBC program. Note that embedded SQL looks like a "higher level" language; that is, it can be coded with less attention to housekeeping details and with some constructs, such as *exec sql whenever*, that may ease the programmer's task and are not present in ODBC. Just as you can convert a program in a high level language (such as C) to a low level one (such as assembler), you can go from embedded SQL to ODBC fairly mechanically.

The reverse — taking ODBC code and translating it to embedded SQL — is possible too. Here, for instance, is an example from the source code of a hypothetical driver which is called as ODBC and implemented as embedded SQL:

```
/* This excerpt can process an SqlExecDirect call provided that
the argument is passed as a null-terminated string and that it
doesn't contain a SELECT */
RETCODE SQL_API SQLEXECDIRECT (
    HSTMT hstmt,
    UCHAR FAR *szSqlStr,
    SDWORD cbSqlStr)
{
if (cbSqlStr!=SQL_NTS) return (-1);
if (strncmpi(szSqlStr,6,"SELECT")==0) return (-1);
exec sql execute immediate :szSqlStr;
if (sqlcode<0) return (-1);
return (0); }
```

# So How is it All Done?

The ODBC architecture has four components:

☐ *The Application Program*, which is responsible for the processing. It calls ODBC functions to send SQL statements to a database and retrieve the results.

☐ *The Driver Manager*, which is responsible for loading ODBC drivers for the application. The Driver Manager is provided by Microsoft.

☐ *The ODBC Driver*, which is responsible for processing the ODBC calls found in the application program. It submits SQL requests to a specific data source, and returns the results to the application program. The ODBC Driver is normally provided by a third party vendor; most often the vendor that also provided the DBMS the driver is associated with.

☐ *The Data Source* itself.

There are lots more things that we could say about ODBC: what's actually in the "driver manager" package that you can get from Microsoft, how well the various ODBC drivers and ODBC clients get along with each other, the details of installing and maintaining, and of course the details about all the calls, core and non-core, that we didn't get into here.

These are all vital questions for administrators and advanced programmers. However, since our space is limited, instead of broadening the discussion, we're going to deepen it: the next section of this chapter takes an in-depth look at how the ODBC core function calls can be used in a real program.

## *An ODBC Program*

We will now throw you into the ODBC lake and see if you swim.

The lake is an ODBC program, Listing 5.3, which is a complete C program with a real-world purpose. It takes data from an ODBC driver and exports it to a dBASE-compatible (*.DBF*) file. The program has fewer than 200 lines of actual code, but we've added lots of drown-proofing in the form of comments.

It's premature to say, "This is good ODBC programming style." These are early days and no style is established. But if it's not presumptuous, we'll suggest that what we present in Listing 5.3 is a reasonable model to follow for C programming. (In C++, various ideas exist for putting wrappers around the boring cycle of "call SQL function | check for error"; also we'd expect that, since the various functions are so clearly demarcable into phases, a higher ordering is possible.)

You'll find this program, in two different versions, on the diskette that comes with this book. *ODBF_DOS.C* is the MS-DOS version, and *ODBF_WIN.C* is the Windows version. Batch files for compiling and linking these programs are also present on the diskette. *ODBF_DOS.C* and *ODBF_WIN.C* use a demo ODBC driver library, which is also supplied.

## Listing 5.3

```
/* This program exports to a .DBF file from an SQL database, using
ODBC v1.0, with host language = Borland C 3.1 large model. */

/* We start with the usual list of C #include files. If you use a
different C compiler, the names may differ. These #include files
contain prototypes for the standard-library C functions: close(),
exit(), free(), gets(), lseek(), malloc(), memset(), open(), printf(),
strchr(), strcpy(), write().*/

#include <stdio.h>
#include <string.h>
#include <stdlib.h>
#include <io.h>
#include <dos.h>
#include <fcntl.h>
#include <mem.h>
#include <sys\stat.h>
#include <ctype.h>

/* The main difference between the MS-DOS and Windows versions of this
program is that the Windows version contains '#include "windows.h"' as
the next line, and does not contain the following five lines, since
FALSE and TRUE and FAR and PASCAL are defined in "windows.h", and since
the stack checking differs between the MS-DOS and Windows versions of
the ODBC driver. */

#define FALSE 0
#define TRUE 1
#define FAR far
#define PASCAL pascal
extern unsigned _stklen = 30000;        /* a big stack, Borland-specific
*/

/* The include file for the ODBC core functions
SQL.H is the include file that comes with the Microsoft kit, and
generally the following line of code would be: #include "sql.h". The
program on the disk that comes with this book will contain a different
name here because it is not a Microsoft product. */

#include "sql.h"
```

# Listing 5.3 — continued

```
/* Because __SQL is already defined in sql.h, all the lines between
"##ifndef __SQL" and "#endif" are comments. But we want to expose all
the sql.h definitions and equations we actually use in this program. So
the following #define's and typedef's and function prototypes are all
taken from sql.h. About 200 lines in all. */

#ifndef __SQL
#define __SQL
#define SQL_NTS              -3  /* In most ODBC functions, when strings
                                    are passed, a length parameter
                                    is passed too. This program uses a
                                    special value for length parameters:
                                    SQL_NTS "Null Terminated String",
                                    to indicate that strings end with \0.*/
#define SQL_SQLSTATE_SIZE     5  /* The "state" of the last SQL
                                    command is how it came out: with
                                    an Error, a Warning, or OK. The
                                    specific state, SQLSTATE, is a
                                    5-byte alphanumeric string (\0 not
                                    included); the size required by ANSI.
                                    Microsoft defines 57 possible values;
                                    the driver maker can define more*/
#define SQL_MAX_MESSAGE_LENGTH 512/* Messages must have a fixed maximum
                                    size. 512 is a bit small but
                                    it's what comes with the package.*/
#define SQL_MAX_DSN_LENGTH    32 /* Maximum length of the "Data
                                    Source Name". Again, a bit small
                                    (it would be nice if it equalled the
                                    maximum length of a path name), but
                                    it's what comes with the package. */


/* THE POSSIBLE RETURN CODES FROM CALLING SQL FUNCTIONS. These are
RETCODEs, which we'll define later with "typedef int." As in embedded
SQL, errors are negative, warnings are positive, and OK is 0 -- but
that's all you find out from a RETCODE. The details about an error are
in SQLSTATE */
```

# Listing 5.3 — continued

```
#define SQL_ERROR              -1  /* e.g., SQL syntax is bad      */
#define SQL_INVALID_HANDLE     -2  /* forgot SQLAllocEnv etc.?     */
#define SQL_NO_DATA_FOUND     100  /* e.g., if a FETCH fails       */
#define SQL_SUCCESS             0  /* "OK"                         */
#define SQL_SUCCESS_WITH_INFO   1  /* "OK but there's a warning"   */


/* SQLFreeStmt has other options, SQL_DROP is the only one we use here.*/

#define SQL_DROP               1


/* Following are all the "core" SQL data types (dates, timestamps and
bits are "non-core" data types, and so are not supported by all ODBC
drivers). We haven't considered the possibility that there might be a
double-byte character set. The numbers are defined by ANSI. */


#define SQL_CHAR     1 /* ANSI definition: "fixed length string"  */
#define SQL_NUMERIC  2 /* ANSI definition: "exact numeric,
                          true precision = defined precision"     */
#define SQL_DECIMAL  3 /* ANSI definition: "exact numeric,
                          true precision >= defined precision"    */
#define SQL_INTEGER  4 /* 32-bit signed integer                   */
#define SQL_SMALLINT 5 /* 16-bit signed integer                   */
#define SQL_FLOAT    6 /* ANSI definition: "approximate numeric,
                          binary precision >= defined precision"  */
#define SQL_REAL     7 /* ANSI definition: "approximate numeric,
                          implementor defined precision"          */
#define SQL_DOUBLE   8 /* ANSI definition: "approximate numeric,
                          implementor defined precision > REAL"   */
#define SQL_VARCHAR 12 /* ANSI definition: "varying length string */


/* When we describe how data can be fetched using the SQLBindCol()
function, we can specify what C data type the ODBC driver should
automatically convert to. In this program, we convert all SQL data types
to C strings so the only type we have to know is SQL_C_CHAR, meaning,
"ASCII string ending with \0". Actually, there is no other kind of CHAR.*/


#define SQL_C_CHAR    SQL_CHAR   /* CHAR, VARCHAR, DECIMAL, NUMERIC */
```

# Listing 5.3 — continued

```
/* If we "fetch" a NULL value, then the length of the returned variable
equals SQL_NULL_DATA. Compare the use of indicator variables in
embedded SQL. */

#define SQL_NULL_DATA    -1

/* Suppose we attempt to allocate an Environment Handle using the
function henv=SQLAllocEnv(). If we fail, the handle's NULL innit?
Frankly we'd just as soon check "if (henv==NULL)" but "if
(henv==SQL_NULL_HENV)" must be what Microsoft recommends, since it's in
sql.h. We'll go along with that. */

#define SQL_NULL_HENV    0    /* null Handle of ENVironment         */
#define SQL_NULL_HDBC    0    /* null Handle of DataBase Connection*/
#define SQL_NULL_HSTMT   0    /* null Handle of STateMenT           */

/* Following are the "SQL portable types." Define your variables with
these names, instead of the original C type, if the variable will be
passed to/from ODBC, e.g., 'UWORD u;' instead of 'unsigned short int u;'.
Portable typing's advantage is that when you switch from a 16-bit to a
32-bit C compiler the meaning of the word 'int' changes, but you can ensure
that the meaning of SWORD remains the same by adjusting only one line here.*/

/* C TYPE                    PORTABLE      STANDS
                             TYPE          FOR
                             NAME */

typedef unsigned char        UCHAR;        /* "Unsigned CHAR"        */
typedef signed char          SCHAR;        /* "Signed CHAR"          */
typedef long int             SDWORD;       /* "Signed Double Word"   */
typedef short int            SWORD;        /* "Signed Word"          */
typedef unsigned long int    UDWORD;       /* "Unsigned Double Word" */
typedef unsigned short int   UWORD;        /* "Unsigned Word"        */
typedef double               SDOUBLE;      /* "Signed Double Real"   */
typedef long double          LDOUBLE;      /* "Long Double Real"     */
typedef float                SFLOAT;       /* "Signed Float"         */

typedef void FAR *           PTR;
```

## Listing 5.3 — continued

```
/* The environment, the database connection and the statement are three
items that all working ODBC programs have handles to. */

typedef void FAR *          HENV;    /* handle of environment      */
typedef void FAR *          HDBC;    /* handle of database connection*/
typedef void FAR *          HSTMT;   /* handle of statement        */


/* All ODBC functions are called the same way and return the same way:
int pascal far SQLAllocConnect (...) */

typedef int                 RETCODE;

/* environment specific definitions */

#define SQL_API PASCAL FAR

/* THE PROTOTYPES OF THE ODBC CORE FUNCTIONS WE USE
In this program we use 15 ODBC functions, called "core" functions because
they're fundamental and will be supported by all ODBC drivers. They fall
into four quite separate groups, depending what phase we're in. In order
of their appearance in the program, the phases and their functions are:

Phase I -- initialization. The 4 functions are SQLAllocEnv(),
SQLAllocConnect(), SQLConnect(), and SQLAllocStmt().

Phase II -- prepare, and check preparation results. The word "prepare"
is used to combine the two ordinary terms "parse and bind." The 3
functions are SQLPrepare(), SQLNumResultCols(), and  SQLDescribeCol().

Phase III-- execution, with ancillary functions telling the ODBC driver
where to put things. The 3 functions are SQLBindCol(),  SQLExecute()
and SQLFetch().

Phase IV -- reverse the initialization done in Phase I. The 4 functions
are SQLFreeStmt(), SQLDisconnect(), SQLFreeConnect(), and  SQLFreeEnv().

The 15th function appears throughout: SQLError() gets error information.*/
```

## Listing 5.3 — continued

```
RETCODE SQL_API SQLAllocEnv(
HENV     FAR   *phenv);       /* point to environment handle    */

RETCODE SQL_API SQLAllocConnect(
HENV            henv,         /* environment handle             */
HDBC     FAR   *phdbc);       /* point to connection handle     */

RETCODE SQL_API SQLConnect(
HDBC            hdbc,         /* connection handle              */
UCHAR    FAR   *szDSN,        /* pointer to data source name    */
SWORD           cbDSN,        /* length of data source name     */
UCHAR    FAR   *szUID,        /* pointer to user identifier      */
SWORD           cbUID,        /* length of user identifier      */
UCHAR    FAR   *szAuthStr,    /* "authentication" e.g., password*/
SWORD           cbAuthStr);   /* length of authentication       */

RETCODE SQL_API SQLAllocStmt(
HDBC            hdbc,         /* connection handle              */
HSTMT    FAR   *phstmt);      /* point to statement handle      */

RETCODE SQL_API SQLPrepare(
HSTMT           hstmt,        /* statement handle               */
UCHAR    FAR   *szSqlStr,     /* SQL text string                */
SDWORD          cbSqlStr);    /* length of SQL text string      */

RETCODE SQL_API SQLNumResultCols(
HSTMT           hstmt,        /* statement handle               */
SWORD    FAR   *pccol);       /* number of columns in result set*/

RETCODE SQL_API SQLDescribeCol(
HSTMT           hstmt,        /* statement handle               */
UWORD           icol,         /* column number, base 1          */
UCHAR    FAR   *szColName,    /* column name                    */
SWORD           cbColNameMax, /* max length of column name      */
SWORD    FAR   *pcbColName,   /* returned length of column name */
SWORD    FAR   *pfSqlType,    /* SQL data type, e.g., SQL_CHAR  */
UDWORD   FAR   *pcbColDef,    /* precision                      */
SWORD    FAR   *pibScale,     /* scale                          */
SWORD    FAR   *pfNullable);  /*e.g., SQL_NULLABLE nulls allowed*/
```

# Listing 5.3 — continued

```
RETCODE SQL_API SQLBindCol(
HSTMT            hstmt,        /* statement handle             */
UWORD           icol,         /* column number, base 1        */
SWORD           fCType,       /* C data type, e.g., SQL_C_CHAR */
PTR             rgbValue,     /* point to data                */
SDWORD          cbValueMax,   /* max length of rgbValue       */
SDWORD    FAR   *pcbValue);   /* point to length of data      */

RETCODE SQL_API SQLExecute(
HSTMT            hstmt);       /* statement handle             */

RETCODE SQL_API SQLFetch(
HSTMT            hstmt);       /* statement handle             */

RETCODE SQL_API SQLFreeStmt(
HSTMT            hstmt,        /* statement handle             */
UWORD           fOption);     /* e.g., SQL_DROP               */

RETCODE SQL_API SQLDisconnect(
HDBC            hdbc);         /* connection handle            */

RETCODE SQL_API SQLFreeConnect(
HDBC            hdbc);         /* connection handle            */

RETCODE SQL_API SQLFreeEnv(
HENV            henv);         /* environment handle           */

RETCODE SQL_API SQLError(
HENV            henv,         /* environment handle           */
HDBC            hdbc,         /* connection handle            */
HSTMT           hstmt,        /* statement handle             */
UCHAR     FAR   *szSqlState,  /* state ret'd by last SQL command*/
SDWORD    FAR   *pfNativeError,/* error code ret'd by data source*/
UCHAR     FAR   *szErrorMsg,  /* error message text           */
SWORD           cbErrorMsgMax,/* max length of error message  */
SWORD     FAR   *pcbErrorMsg);/* ret'd length of error message */

#endif                        /* #ifndef __SQL                */

/* End of definitions taken from "sql.h" */
```

## Listing 5.3 — continued

```
/* Prototypes for all three routines in the body of this program */

void main ();
int export (UCHAR *database, UCHAR *sql_statement, char *dbf_filename);
int errcheck (UCHAR *msg,RETCODE rc,HENV henv,HDBC hdbc,HSTMT hstmt);

/* Field names in .DBF files are 11 bytes long, SQL column names are
generally 18 characters long. */

#define DBFNAMESIZE 11
#define SQLNAMESIZE 18

/* THE .DBF HEADER
The main type of dBASE-compatible file, called a .DBF file because the
normal extension is "*.DBF," has a reasonably well-established form:
-- First comes the "file header" (dbf_header).
-- Then come the "field headers" (field_header), one per field.
-- Then comes the actual data, in fixed-field format.
The following 'struct header' defines the file header and field
headers together.

Explanation of struct dbf_header: dbf_header_version has various flags mark-
ing the type of file (we'll skip the complications and say that a value of 3
means "dBASE-III-like with no memos; dbf_header_update is a year-month-day
field with the last time the file was changed (we'll put in a fixed value
here); dbf_header_recordcount is the number of records in the file;
dbf_header_size is the length of the header plus the length of all the field
headers; dbf_header_record_size is the length of each record; dbf_header_re-
serve and dbf_header_pending etc. don't really matter for our purposes.

Explanation of struct field_header:  fieldheader_name contains the name
of the field with trailing \0s and the last (eleventh) byte must be \0;
dbf_fieldheader_type can be 'C' for Character, 'N' for Number as an
ASCII number including digits or . or - (other possibilities are 'D'
date, 'F' float, 'L' Logical, and 'M' Memo but this program only
produces 'C' or 'N'); fieldheader_address will be used for storing the
address but we write a fake value in the file; dbf_fieldheader_size is
the displayable size; and dbf_fieldheader_decimal is the number of
positions after the decimal point; the rest doesn't matter here (we use
some reserve fields as scratch space, though). */
```

## Listing 5.3 — continued

```
struct dbf_header {
    char dbf_header_version;
    char dbf_header_last_update[3];
    unsigned long dbf_header_recordcount;
    unsigned dbf_header_size;
    unsigned dbf_header_record_size;
    char dbf_header_reserve1[2];
    char dbf_header_pending;
    char dbf_header_reserve2[13];
    char dbf_header_mdx;
    char dbf_header_reserve3[3];
    struct field_header {
        char dbf_fieldheader_name[DBFNAMESIZE];
        char dbf_fieldheader_type;
        long dbf_fieldheader_address;
        unsigned char dbf_fieldheader_size;
        unsigned char dbf_fieldheader_decimal;
        unsigned char dbf_fieldheader_reserve1[2];
        unsigned char dbf_fieldheader_flag;
        unsigned char dbf_fieldheader_reserve2[10];
        char dbf_fieldheader_mdx; }
    ff[1]; };

/* THE main() FUNCTION
main() gets information typed in by the user, calls export(), and re-
turns. Although we use 'printf()' and 'gets()', all the major C
compilers have libraries which allow the running of such programs un-
der Windows without modification. */

void main ()
{
char sql_statement[25];
char database[SQL_MAX_DSN_LENGTH+1];  /*i.e., 32 according to sql.h */
char dbf_filename[25];                /* maximum path size?          */

printf("Type in the name of the database you are importing from\n");
gets(database);

printf("Type in a SQL 'SELECT' statement for the rows you want exported\n");
gets(sql_statement);
```

# Listing 5.3 — continued

```
printf("Type in the name of the .DBF file you are exporting to\n");
gets(dbf_filename);

exit(export(database,sql_statement,dbf_filename)); }

/* export() does all the work, it's called from main(), it calls errcheck() */


int export (UCHAR *database, UCHAR *sql_statement, char *dbf_filename)
{
struct dbf_header *Head = NULL;   /* address of in-RAM .DBF header   */
int file_fd = -1;                 /* set by create()                 */
unsigned int dbf_header_size;     /* total size of field header table*/
int i,j,k;
SWORD ccol;                       /* passed back by SQLNumResultCols */
UWORD icol;                       /* 'current col #', used in loops  */
char c;

RETCODE        rc;

/* There are always at least 3 handles: one for the environment, one
for the database connection, and one for the statement connection.
ODBC allows multiple database connections and multiple (possibly syn-
chronously running) statements, but this program doesn't need that.*/

HENV           henv = SQL_NULL_HENV;  /* env handle, initialized to 0 */
HDBC           hdbc = SQL_NULL_HDBC;  /* dbc handle, initialized to 0 */
HSTMT          hstmt = SQL_NULL_HSTMT;/* stmt handle, initialized to 0*/

UCHAR          *dbf_record = NULL;  /* points to malloc'd record buffer*/
unsigned int   dbf_recordsize;
UCHAR          szColName[SQLNAMESIZE+1];/* returned from SQLDescribeCol */
SWORD          cbColName;           /* returned from SQLDescribeCol   */
SWORD          fSqlType;            /* returned from SQLDescribeCol   */
SWORD          colscale;            /* returned from SQLDescribeCol   */
SWORD          colnullable;         /*ret'd from SQLDescribeCol, unused*/
UDWORD         collen;              /* ret'd from SQLDescribeCol etc.  */
UCHAR          *colvalue;
UCHAR          *p;
int            _offset;
int            success_fail = FALSE;/* what we return to main()       */
```

## Listing 5.3 — continued

```
/* PHASE I: INITIALIZATION */

/* STANDARD ODBC INITIALIZATION CODE All functional ODBC programs always
contain these statements in this order: SQLAllocEnv(), SQLAllocConnect(),
SQLConnect(), SQLAllocStmt(). So, unless you need multiple connections
and multiple statements at the same time, the following code is boilerplate.

Essentially, the SQLAlloc... functions merely cause the ODBC driver to
allocate internal space for storing semi-permanent information. Probably
the ODBC driver malloc's a bit of RAM for storing pointers to the other
handles and the most recent error messages, and (for the connection
handle) the name of the database, or (for the statement handle) the
text of the last SQL statement, the position within a cursor, etc.

Take note: The three SQLAlloc... functions all return 32-bit "handles."
Some ODBC drivers are actually returning pointers to the ODBC driver's
semi-permanent information. To test for this, after initialization try
casting hstmt to a PTR ("p = (PTR) hstmt") and then see if accessing *p
results in a General Protection Fault with Windows 3.1. If not, you can
peek at the structure that the ODBC driver dynamically allocates when you
call SQLAllocStmt().

The SQLConnect() function establishes a connection to a data source. A
"data source" is probably just a "database," as we can see from the fact
that "hdbc," according to Microsoft, stands for "handle to database
connection." So our SQLConnect(...,"SYSADM",...""",...) call just means
"open up <database> with userid='SYSADM', no password".

Notice that we always follow ODBC function calls with a call to an
error-checking routine. In this phase, errors would most likely be due
to insufficient memory, failure to find a file, or network failure. */

rc=SQLAllocEnv(&henv);
if (errcheck("SQLAllocEnv",rc,henv,hdbc,hstmt)) goto cleanup;

rc=SQLAllocConnect(henv,&hdbc);
if (errcheck("SQLAllocConnect",rc,henv,hdbc,hstmt)) goto cleanup;

rc=SQLConnect(hdbc,database,SQL_NTS,"SYSADM",SQL_NTS,"",SQL_NTS);
if (errcheck("SQLConnect",rc,henv,hdbc,hstmt)) goto cleanup;
```

# Listing 5.3 — continued

```
rc=SQLAllocStmt(hdbc,&hstmt);
if (errcheck("SQLAllocStmt",rc,henv,hdbc,hstmt)) goto cleanup;

/* PHASE II: PREPARATION */

/* PREPARE THE SELECT STATEMENT. Initialization is complete, we've done
the SQLAlloc...() calls, and we've opened the database. Now it's time to
look at the SELECT statement that the user typed in. We don't actually
execute the SELECT statement yet -- first we have to check if it's a
valid statement, and then we'll do some preparatory work based on the
description of the columns being selected. */

rc=SQLPrepare(hstmt,sql_statement,SQL_NTS);
if (errcheck("SQLPrepare",rc,henv,hdbc,hstmt)) goto cleanup;

/* GET THE NUMBER OF COLUMNS. We've initialized and we've run the user's
SELECT statement through SQLPrepare(). Now some information is
available: specifically, how many columns were in the SELECT (which we
can now retrieve with the SQLNumResultCols() function), and what the
datatype, size, and name of each column is (which we will soon retrieve
with the SQLDescribeCol() function).

Find out how many columns were in the SELECT that we just SQLPrepared.
If it wasn't a SELECT, then SQLNumResultCols should set ccol=0. If the
number is greater than the maximum number of fields allowed by some
packages, display a warning but continue. */

/* "Let ccol = the number of columns in the SELECT that we SQLPrepared()"*/

rc = SQLNumResultCols(hstmt, &ccol);
if (errcheck("SQLNumResultCols",rc,henv,hdbc,hstmt)) goto cleanup;
if (ccol == 0) {
    printf("Error: there were no result columns in the SQL statement\n");
    printf("you typed. Either the statement was not legal, or it wasn't a\n");
    printf("SELECT statement (this program won't process INSERT,\n");
    printf("DELETE, etc.).\n");
    goto cleanup; }
if (ccol>128) {
    printf("Warning: Some variants of dBASE and its clones cannot handle\n");
    printf("databases with more than 128 fields. We will be setting up a\n");
    printf("database with %d fields.\n",ccol); }
```

# Listing 5.3 — continued

```
/* ALLOCATE SPACE FOR THE HEADER OF THE .DBF FILE. We need enough for
the file header, each of the field headers, and one extra byte at the
end. (Some packages put TWO bytes at the end; consistency's tough when
there's no standard.)*/

dbf_header_size=
sizeof(struct dbf_header)+(ccol-1)*sizeof(struct field_header)+1;
Head = malloc(dbf_header_size);
if (Head == NULL) {
    printf("The malloc() function failed, the file header can't be set up\n");
    goto cleanup; }
memset(Head,0,dbf_header_size);        /* initialize header to all \0s */

/* SET VALUES IN THE .DBF FILE HEADER. The dbf_header_size value will be
the number of bytes in the file header plus all the field headers; the
version will be 3, meaning "dBASE III made this"; the date field will be
October 1 1993 (we're avoiding Borland's "getdate(&cdate)" because it's
vendor-specific; the date here really doesn't matter); dbf_header_recordcount
will be filled in later; dbf_header_reserve1, dbf_header_pending,
dbf_header_reserve2, dbf_header_mdx and on the diskette that comes
with this book dbf_header_reserve3 all remain equal to 0. */



Head->dbf_header_size=dbf_header_size;
Head->dbf_header_version=0x3;
Head->dbf_header_last_update[0]=93;    /* year */
Head->dbf_header_last_update[1]=10;    /* mon */
Head->dbf_header_last_update[2]=01;    /* day */

/* SET VALUES IN EACH OF THE .DBF FIELD HEADERS. This is done in a loop,
ccol times (remember that ccol is the number of columns, as we found out
from our call to the SQLNumResultCols() function). The key ODBC function
that we need for finding information about columns is the
SQLDescribeCol() function. We have a few trivial problems to solve
afterwards because the SQL description which we retrieve with
SQLDescribeCol() has names and types that don't have exact equivalents
in a .DBF description.
```

# Listing 5.3 — continued

In a general way, the loop is equivalent to the "exec sql DESCRIBE"
statement found in embedded SQL. */

```
/* Head->dbf_header_record_size=1; */

for (icol=0,_offset=0; icol<ccol; ++icol) {
    rc = SQLDescribeCol(hstmt,
    icol + 1,       /* "Given the column number, base 1,              */
    szColName,      /* return the column name                        */
    SQLNAMESIZE,    /* (noting that the maximum name length is 18),   */
    &cbColName,     /* return the size of the column name,            */
    &fSqlType,      /* return the type, e.g., SQL_CHAR, SQL_INTEGER   */
    &collen,        /* return the precision ('length' if SqlType=CHAR), */
    &colscale,      /* return the scale (0 if scale is not applicable), */
    &colnullable);/* and return "nullability", which we'll ignore." */
    if (errcheck("SQLDescribeCol",rc,henv,hdbc,hstmt)) goto cleanup;

/* SQLDescribeCol put the length of the SQL column name in cbColName
and the actual column name in szColName. Put the SQL column name in
the .DBF field header item [icol].dbf_fieldheader. */

    if (cbColName > DBFNAMESIZE - 1) {
    /* Alternative: check if rc=SQL_SUCCESS_WITH_INFO && sqlstate="01004" */
        printf("Warning: the SQL column name %s contains %d\n",cbColName);
        printf("characters. The maximum width of a column name in a name in\n");
        printf("a .DBF field header is %d.\n",DBFNAMESIZE-1);
        cbColName=DBFNAMESIZE - 1; }
    for (i=0; i<cbColName; ++i) {
      if (!isalnum(szColName[i])) {
        printf("Warning: the SQL column name %s contains\n");
        printf("one or\n",szColName);
        printf("more non-alphanumeric characters. Such names may not\n");
        printf("be accepted in field headers by all dBASE-like products.\n");
        break; } }
    strncpy(Head->ff[icol].dbf_fieldheader_name,szColName,cbColName);
```

# Listing 5.3 — continued

```c
/* SQLDescribeCol put the type of the SQL column in fSqlType, and the
length (or numeric precision) of the SQL column in collen. If the SQL
type is CHAR or VARCHAR, then the .DBF field header type is 'C' and the
.DBF size is the same as the SQL size. Otherwise, the .DBF fieldheader
type is 'N' and the size is the maximum number of displayable
characters. For instance, SQL_INTEGERs are 32 bits and signed, so the
largest possible number is -2147483648, which is 11 bytes wide. With
SQL_DECIMAL, "." and "-" are not included in SQL's precision+scale, but
are included for a .DBF, since the .DBF's size is the count of
displayable characters.*/

if (fSqlType==SQL_CHAR || fSqlType==SQL_VARCHAR) {
    Head->ff[icol].dbf_fieldheader_type='C'; }  /* SQL char --> dbf 'C'*/
else {
    if (fSqlType==SQL_INTEGER) collen=12;        /* max=-2147483648   */
    else if (fSqlType==SQL_SMALLINT) collen=6;  /* max=-32767         */
    else if (fSqlType==SQL_DECIMAL) collen+=2;  /* include for "-" and "."*/
    else if (fSqlType==SQL_FLOAT) ;
    else {
        printf("Column %s has a 'non-core' data type.\n",szColName);
        printf("The only data types we can process are INTEGER,\n");
        printf("SMALLINT, DECIMAL, FLOAT, CHAR and\n");
        printf("VARCHAR.\n");
        goto cleanup; }
    Head->ff[icol].dbf_fieldheader_type='N'; }

if (collen>255) {
    printf("Warning: Column %s is %d bytes wide.\n",szColName,collen);
    printf("Many dBASE-compatible products cannot handle a column\n");
    printf("wider than 255. But some can, so we'll continue without\n");
    printf("truncating.\n"); }

Head->ff[icol].dbf_fieldheader_size=collen;
Head->ff[icol].dbf_fieldheader_decimal=colscale;
Head->dbf_header_record_size+=collen;
Head->ff[icol].dbf_fieldheader_address=0x516b000d+_offset;
_offset+=Head->ff[icol].dbf_fieldheader_size;
Head->ff[icol].dbf_fieldheader_flag=1;
```

## Listing 5.3 — continued

```
/* dbf_fieldheader_reserve1 and dbf_fieldheader_reserve2 and
dbf_fieldheader_mdx all remain 0 */ }
```

```
/* CREATE THE .DBF FILE AND WRITE THE HEADER. As a result of our call to
SQLNumResultCols() and the loop that came after it with the
SQLDescribeCol() function, we now have all the information we need for a
.DBF header -- dbf_header has the general data, field_headers have the
dope on each field (name, size, type, etc.). We don't yet know the
number of rows, but we intend to come back later and fill in the
number-of-rows field when we've finished. */
```

```
file_fd=open(dbf_filename,
O_CREAT|O_RDWR|O_BINARY|O_TRUNC,S_IREAD|S_IWRITE);
if (file_fd<0) {
    printf("The open() function failed, the .DBF file can't be created\n");
    goto cleanup; }
```

```
if (write(file_fd,Head,dbf_header_size)!=dbf_header_size) {
    printf("The write() function failed, the .DBF header can't be written\n");
    goto cleanup; }
```

```
/* PHASE III: EXECUTION */
```

```
/* ALLOCATE A RECORD BUFFER TO FETCH DATA INTO AND WRITE DATA FROM. The
record buffer is what we write to the .DBF file. Within the record
buffer is the space for each field. The size of each field was figured
out earlier; it's still in the field header (dbf_fieldheader_size). We
believe it's slightly more efficient to have just one record buffer,
rather than a separate buffer for each field.
```

```
The key ODBC function call in the following loop is SQLBindCol(), which
tells the driver what address to fetch column values into and what
conversions to perform. In this case, we tell it to convert to
SQL_C_CHAR i.e., \0-terminated strings regardless of original type;
that's because a .DBF file contains nothing but ASCII data. */
```

# Listing 5.3 — continued

```
dbf_recordsize = Head->dbf_header_record_size + 1;
dbf_record = (void *) malloc(dbf_recordsize + 1);
if (dbf_record == NULL) {
    printf("A malloc() function failed, the record buffer can't be set up\n");
    goto cleanup; }
for (icol=0,colvalue=dbf_record+1; icol<ccol; ++icol) {
    Head->ff[icol].dbf_fieldheader_address=(long)colvalue;
    collen=Head->ff[icol].dbf_fieldheader_size;

/* colvalue points to where we'll fetch data for this field, i.e., for
field number [icol+1], when we call the SQLFetch() function later;
collen is the maximum amount of data that we can fetch for the field
(which should be OK since it equals the defined size); the final
parameter for SQLBindCol() tells it where to put a column's "indicator"
value.*/

    rc = SQLBindCol(hstmt,icol+1,SQL_C_CHAR,colvalue,collen,
    (SDWORD*)Head->ff[icol].dbf_fieldheader_reserve2);
    if (errcheck("BindCol",rc,henv,hdbc,hstmt)) goto cleanup;
    colvalue+=collen; }

/* Set the first byte of the record buffer to blank to indicate it's
not deleted (a 'deleted' record in a .DBF file is represented by 0x2a
in the first byte). */

*dbf_record=' ';

/* ACTUALLY DO THE SELECT STATEMENT.
This is "part II" of SQL-statement processing. In part I we call the
SQLPrepare() function to check the statement out and find out about its
characteristics and effects; in part II we call SQLExecute() to actually
perform the statement. (The two steps can be combined using the ODBC
function SQLExecDirect(), which we don't illustrate in this program.)

We could have called SQLExecute() immediately after SQLPrepare(), and
then set up the .DBF header. Instead, we called SQLPrepare(), then we
set up the .DBF header, and now we're going to call SQLExecute(). Our
idea is that executing a SQL statement is a use of precious system (or
network) resources; therefore if anything can go wrong with the .DBF
setup then we may as well find out in advance, so that we can skip
processing the SELECT. It's a minor design point.
```

## Listing 5.3 — continued

Anyway, the ODBC driver stored the prepared SELECT statement in the
handle referenced by hstmt, so now we just have to invoke it. */

```
rc = SQLExecute(hstmt);
if (errcheck("SQLExecute",rc,henv,hdbc,hstmt)) goto cleanup;
```

/* THE MAIN LOOP -- FETCH SQL ROWS, WRITE .DBF RECORDS.
We've initialized the ODBC interface (including connecting to the database),
we've opened the .DBF file for output and set up the .DBF header
information based on information we got about the SQL statement's
columns, and we've actually executed the SQL statement, so now all the
rows we've asked for are waiting for us in what's called a "result set."
All we have to do is get data from the result set using the ODBC
SQLFetch() function and dump the data into the .DBF file using good old
write(), one row at a time until SQLFetch() tells us there are no more
rows. */

```
for (;;) {
      /* We're ready to get the next row of the result set with
SQLFetch().*/
      rc = SQLFetch(hstmt);
      if (errcheck("SQLFetch",rc,henv,hdbc,hstmt)) goto cleanup;
      if (rc==SQL_NO_DATA_FOUND) break;
```

/* The SQLFetch() succeeded, so now the record buffer is filled with
data. Remember our call to the SqlNumResultCols() function? That's when
we set ccol to the number of columns in each row of the result set.
Remember our calls to SQLBindCol()? They established the address of
each column's data (pointed to by ...[icol].dbf_fieldheader_address in
the field header) and we use other items in the field header --
[icol].dbf_fieldheader_size, [icol].dbf_fieldheader_type -- to do the
final massaging of that data: space filling, null substitution, and
right justification. */

```
      for (icol=0; icol<ccol; ++icol) {
            memmove(&collen,Head->ff[icol].dbf_fieldheader_reserve2,
            sizeof(SDWORD));
            colvalue=(UCHAR*)Head->ff[icol].dbf_fieldheader_address;
            if (collen==SQL_NULL_DATA) {
                collen=0;
```

## Listing 5.3 — continued

```
/* collen == -1, meaning the SQL column had a NULL at this location.
Since dBASE doesn't support NULLs, there's no official way to store them
in .DBF files. We'll act as if the field is blank. That's consistent
with the way that, e.g., XDB's export-to-DBF utility does it.*/ }

/* The data *colvalue is SQL_C_CHAR, so it's \0-terminated. That's not
how we want to store it: a .DBF file is always fixed field. If
it's a Character field ('C'), space fill on the right. If it's a
Numeric field ('N'), right-justify and space fill on the left.*/

    i=Head->ff[icol].dbf_fieldheader_size; /* i="defined size" */
    if (Head->ff[icol].dbf_fieldheader_type=='C') {
        memset(colvalue+collen,' ',i-collen); }
    else {
        strncpy(colvalue+i-collen,colvalue,collen);
        memset(colvalue,' ',i-collen); }

/* Fix the number of zeros after the decimal point, if any. */

    k=Head->ff[icol].dbf_fieldheader_decimal;
    if (k>0) {
        *(colvalue+j)='\0';
        p=strchr(colvalue,'.');
        if (p==0) {
            strcpy(colvalue,colvalue+1);
            p=colvalue+j-1;
            *p='.'; }
        k-=(colvalue+j)-(p+1);
        while (k>0) {
            strcpy(colvalue,colvalue+1);
            *(colvalue+j-1)='0';
            --k; } } }

/* We've massaged all the fields in the record buffer. Now dump the
record buffer to the .DBF file and increment the record count in the
file header buffer. This is the end of the main loop. */
```

# Listing 5.3 — continued

```
    if (write(file_fd,dbf_record,dbf_recordsize)!=dbf_recordsize) {
        printf("The write() function failed, the record can't be written\n");
        goto cleanup; }
    ++Head->dbf_header_recordcount; }

/* There's only one way to get here: we broke out of the SQLFetch()
loop because "if (rc==SQL_NO_DATA_FOUND)" is true, meaning all rows
have been written. At this point some packages write 0x1a (control-Z)
as an "eof" marker. */

/* WRITE THE RECORD COUNT IN THE HEADER.
While we were in the loop we were incrementing Head->dbf_header_recordcount,
so now we know how many rows there are in the file, total. Seek back to
near the start of the .DBF file and rewrite that. The other header
information is unchanged. */

if (lseek(file_fd,4L,0)==-1) {
    printf("The seek() function failed, the record count can't be written\n");
    goto cleanup; }
if (write(file_fd,&Head->dbf_header_recordcount,4)!=4) {
    printf("The write() function failed, the recordcount can't be written\n");
    goto cleanup; }

/* Mark that we're a big success, getting here means we did all the rows. */

success_fail=TRUE;

/* PHASE IV: DE-INITIALIZATION */

cleanup: ;

/* CLEAN UP.
We're done. Now it's time to close the .DBF file, free the buffers
that we malloc'd for the header and record buffer, disconnect
from the database, free the SQL environment and database connection and
statement handles, and return to the caller.
```

## Listing 5.3 — continued

Cleanup is necessary because we are taking up system-wide resources. For example, an ODBC driver might call the Windows function GlobalAlloc() when we called the SQLAllocStmt() function at the start of the program. So now we have to call the SQLFreeStmt() function, which will make the ODBC driver call GlobalFree().

All handles and pointers were initialized to null values. Since we 'goto cleanup' if any error happens, they might still be. For instance, hstmt will still equal SQL_NULL_HSTMT if the SQLConnect() function failed. Anyway: destroy all remaining global objects, in the reverse order of their creation. */

```
if (dbf_record!=NULL) free(dbf_record); /* reverse malloc(dbf_record)*/
if (Head!=NULL) free(Head);             /* reverse malloc(Head)      */
if (file_fd>=0) close(file_fd);         /* reverse open(filename)    */
```

/* Experienced SQL programmers might execute a "ROLLBACK" statement here, as part of the cleanup procedure. If that's your habit, break it. First, you're supposed to avoid "ROLLBACK" even though it's ANSI; the "recommended" ODBC equivalent is "SQLTransact(henv,hdbc,SQL_ROLLBACK);". Second, there is no guarantee that all cursors will be closed by ROLLBACK (even though that's ANSI, too); it depends on a setting named SQL_CURSOR_ROLLBACK_BEHAVIOR which can't be controlled. The correct way to close a cursor is with the SQLFreeStmt() function. Here, we'll use SQLFreeStmt() with the SQL_DROP option. */

```
if (hstmt!=SQL_NULL_HSTMT) {
    rc = SQLFreeStmt(hstmt, SQL_DROP); /* reverse SQLAllocStmt() */
```

/* It's very unlikely that SQLFreeStmt() will fail, given that it's probably merely freeing memory.  All the more reason to check for failure, then: if strange things are happening, the user should be warned of the fact. */

```
    if (errcheck("SQLFreeStmt",rc,henv,hdbc,hstmt)) {
        printf("Continuing.\n"); }
    hstmt=SQL_NULL_HSTMT; }
```

# Listing 5.3 — continued

```
if (hdbc!=SQL_NULL_HDBC) {
    rc = SQLDisconnect(hdbc);          /* reverse SQLConnect()     */
    rc = SQLFreeConnect(hdbc);         /* reverse SQLAllocConnect() */
    if (errcheck("SQLFreeConnect",rc,henv,hdbc,hstmt)) {
        printf("Continuing.\n"); }
    hdbc=SQL_NULL_HDBC; }

if (henv!=SQL_NULL_HENV) {
    rc = SQLFreeEnv(henv);             /* reverse SQLAllocEnv()    */
    if (errcheck("SQLExecute",rc,henv,hdbc,hstmt)) {
        printf("Continuing.\n"); }
    henv=SQL_NULL_HENV; }

/* end of export() function, return TRUE or FALSE to main(). */

return (success_fail); }

/* We call errcheck() after every ODBC function call. If there's any
problem, we want to display whatever information we can get about it.
ODBC's SQLError() function is available for this purpose. It should tell
us a standardized error code -- sqlstate -- and it should give us an
error message, which is probably driver-specific. There's a bunch of
problems here: What if the call to SQLError() itself returns an error?
What if the error-message buffer isn't big enough to hold what
SQLError() returns? What if the error code isn't something we expect?
We've tried to be thorough about our diagnosis, so this error checking
routine is almost as long as the main program! But we didn't think it's
a good idea to skimp on the error checking in a "model" ODBC program.

If all goes well, errcheck() returns FALSE. Otherwise it returns TRUE,
which is a signal to the caller that it's a good idea to smoothly abort.*/

int errcheck (UCHAR *msg,RETCODE rc,HENV henv,HDBC hdbc,HSTMT hstmt)
{
UCHAR   szSqlState[SQL_SQLSTATE_SIZE+1]; /* defined by SAG as = 5   */
SDWORD  pfNativeError;
SWORD   pcbErrorMsg;                      /* gets actual error message size*/
UCHAR   *szErrorMsg;                      /* points to error message buffer*/
SWORD   cbErrorMsgMax = SQL_MAX_MESSAGE_LENGTH;
RETCODE sqlerror_rc;
```

## Listing 5.3 — continued

```
/* Test for three general possibilities: the last function returned
"okay" (i.e., SQL_SUCCESS, SQL_SUCCESS_WITH_INFO, or SQL_NO_DATA_FOUND);
or it returned SQL_ERROR, or it returned something unexpected. */

switch (rc) {
   case SQL_SUCCESS:
   case SQL_SUCCESS_WITH_INFO:
   case SQL_NO_DATA_FOUND:
   return (FALSE);

   case SQL_ERROR:
   printf("The call to function %s() returned SQL_ERROR.\n",msg);
   printf("Calling the SQLError() function to get more information.\n");

nogo: szErrorMsg=malloc(cbErrorMsgMax); /* make a 512-byte message buffer*/
   if (szErrorMsg==NULL) {
      printf("A malloc() failed, can't set up szErrorMsg\n");
      return (TRUE); }

   sqlerror_rc = SQLError(  /* "I want more info about the error:    */
   henv,                    /* From the environment handle, or       */
   hdbc,                    /* from the database-connection handle, or */
   hstmt,                   /* from the statement handle (if not null)*/
   szSqlState,              /* return a \0-terminated 5-byte sqlstate,*/
   &pfNativeError,          /* return the driver's native error code,*/
   szErrorMsg,              /* return the error message text         */
   cbErrorMsgMax            /* (whose maximum size is 512 bytes),    */
   &pcbErrorMsg);           /* and return how big the message is."   */

   switch (sqlerror_rc) {
     case SQL_SUCCESS:
     case SQL_SUCCESS_WITH_INFO:
        printf("A call to SQLError() gives more\n");
        printf("detailed information:\n");
        printf("SqlState = %s.\n",szSqlState);
        printf("Native error code = %ld.\n",pfNativeError);
        printf("Error Message = %s.\n",szErrorMsg);
        if (pcbErrorMsg>cbErrorMsgMax) {
```

## Listing 5.3 — continued

```
/* The message text in szErrorMsg can be as large as
SQL_MAX_MESSAGE_LENGTH, which is defined in SQL.H as 512. But the actual
text that could have been returned is larger than that, as we see by
comparing to pcbErrorMsg. You might think, "Let's increase the message
size and try again," thus: free(szErrorMsg);
                              cbErrorMsgMax=pcbErrorMsg;
                              goto nogo;
BUT! The second call to SQLError() will probably return
SQL_NO_DATA_FOUND; once you call SQLError(), it "removes the error from
the list of available errors." So you have to have a big enough buffer
the first time. */

    printf("Warning: the above error message was truncated\n");
    break;
  default:


/* The call to SQLError() itself resulted in an error. Perhaps it's
SQL_INVALID_HANDLE because henv+hdbc+hstmt are all null -- which would
be the case if SQLAllocEnv() failed. Perhaps it's SQL_NO_DATA_FOUND or
SQL_ERROR, in which case heaven knows why. */

    printf("No further information is available.\n");
    break; }
  free(szErrorMsg);
    return (TRUE); }
default:

/* In this program, it's quite unlikely that any of the SQL function
calls will return anything other than SQL_SUCCESS,
SQL_SUCCESS_WITH_INFO, SQL_NO_DATA_FOUND, or SQL_ERROR. But there are
other theoretical possibilities (SQL_INVALID_HANDLE, SQL_NEED_DATA,
SQL_STILL_EXECUTING) so we have a 'default:' case for completeness.*/

printf("The call to function %s() returned an unexpected\n");
printf("code.\n",msg);
printf("This is probably due to a programming error.\n");
return (TRUE); } }
```

# *Indexing for Performance*

The foundation of a good DBMS's performance is its indexes. All self-respecting DBMS vendors support *CREATE INDEX* and recommend its use. There are a few variations (Ingres, for instance, allows hashing), but most indexes are garden-variety B-trees. An SQL engine might use indexes for any of the following (in order of decreasing likelihood):

1) To solve queries of the form *<column-name> <relator> <value>*, with exceptions for *<>*, *LIKE '%...'*. (Note that we say *<value>* in the singular; an expression with more than one value is rarely used for index-lookup purposes.)

2) To avoid sorts. Sorts are generally fairly expensive and the required time to do a sort grows exponentially with the size of the table. (One of the better types of sort, the partition sort, requires $N*\log_2 N$ comparisons on average, where "N" is the number of rows.) Some vendors have good sort procedures, and some make good use of available RAM. (Find out if taking RAM away from your system has an effect on your SQL engine's sort speed.) But it's generally faster to use a presorted list, and any index is a presorted list. Since the keys of an

index are in order, then ⟨*column-name*⟩ ⟨*relator*⟩ ⟨*value*⟩ will automatically be in order by ⟨*column-name*⟩ if the query is solved by an index. A simple *SELECT* ⟨*column-name*⟩ *FROM* ⟨*table-name*⟩ *ORDER BY* ⟨*column-name*⟩ might also take the keys from the index, though this is far from certain because the index might not have the same value as the original (e.g., it might be uppercase). As well as *ORDER BY*, other clauses imply use of a sort as well: *GROUP BY*, *DISTINCT*, and *UNION*, for example.

3) To handle aggregate functions, especially *MAX*, *MIN*, and *COUNT(DISTINCT)*. Note that:

```
SELECT MAX(COLUMN_B) FROM TABLE_A WHERE COLUMN_A > 5;
```

won't be helped at all by an index on *COLUMN_B*. It's the index on *COLUMN_A*, the column used in the *WHERE* clause, that matters.

4) To ensure that *UNIQUE*, *PRIMARY KEY*, and *FOREIGN KEY* constraints are maintained.

Some vendor-specific variants you might also run into include:

☐ Indexes on joins.

☐ Indexes with particular character sets, based on the *CHARACTER SET IS* option in SQL 92, or on a table for specifying byte value weight, or on the DOS/Windows country code.

☐ Front-truncation (see Chapter 8).

☐ Back-truncation (see Chapter 8) — good for *COLUMN = ⟨UNIQUE-VALUE⟩* queries, but bad for everything else.

☐ Multiple indexes in one file.

☐ Indexes that cluster.

☐ Base tables stored in B-trees.

There are other possibilities: indexes on views, bit-list indexes (becoming a hit with one of the dBASE clone packages), etc. — but to our knowledge none of these have yet appeared in actual SQL implementations.

The DBMS's database catalog will contain information about an index's components and its uniqueness. A few vendors keep information about the index's selectivity (the total number of distinct key values as opposed to the total number of values). Strangely, statistics on actual index usage are not generally an automatic feature.

One item to watch for when creating an index is the maximum size of the index key. Usually the maximum is fixed by the vendor. (We've seen the maximum size vary from 90 to 256 bytes.) Because of this maximum size, it is often not terribly useful to use multiple-column keys — sequential scans will happen anyway because the later indexed columns might not actually be stored in the index.

## *Pros and Cons of Indexing*

When solving a query, an index speeds up selection because it allows the SQL engine to avoid a sequential search (also known as a full table scan). It's well-known that:

```
SELECT * FROM TABLE_A WHERE COLUMN_A = 5;
```

will work faster if *COLUMN_A* has a distributed set of values and there is an index on it, and provided that the number of pages in *TABLE_A*'s tablespace is greater than the number of levels of index (which is generally true if the file contains more than a few thousand bytes). This is because the SQL engine only has to read the top level of index, which points to the next level.

Actually, the engine might not even have to read this many levels because the top levels of index may be so frequently accessed that they're available in a cache. The point, though, is what does *not* happen is a time-consuming pass through *all* the rows in the table.

At the same time, it's clear that:

```
UPDATE TABLE_A SET COLUMN_A = COLUMN_A + COLUMN_B;
```

is much more expensive if *COLUMN_A* is indexed because for each row of *TABLE_A* that we change, we must delete the original index key that pointed to it *and* add a new one elsewhere in the file. In fact, if you have the privilege to do so, you may be better off if you drop the index first, do the update, and then re-create the index. (We have found this true in several cases with respectable DBMSs.)

Indexing speeds up *select*. The price you pay for this optimization is that *insert, update,* and *delete* will be slower. Since *select* is generally more commonly used, and since both *update* and *delete* usually involve a *where* predicate anyway, and since integrity (e.g., primary/unique key) is often enforced by indexes, we feel the price of an index is usually worth paying.

# Indexed Searches

Assume that a disk page is the fixed number of bytes the operating system can read at once. The time needed to read a page is critical, so reducing the number of page reads will improve the system performance. Most DBMSs use a structure called a multi-level index to speed up searches. (Though this structure is technically a B+ tree, it is commonly called a "B-tree" in the database vernacular.)

The leftmost section of Figure 6.1 shows the data records in a table. The table contains 25 records, numbered from 1 to 25 (this number is the physical address). Each record has a one-letter column with a unique value between A and Y. A DBMS can do a sequential search of the table by reading each page in order. Since the values are unique, the DBMS can stop reading when it finds the value it is searching for. Thus, to find A, B, C, D, or E, the DBMS has to read only one page; to find F, G, H, I, or J it must read two pages; to find U, V, W, X, Y it must read five pages. The total is (5*1) + (5*2) + (5*3) + (5*4) + (5*5) = 75 page reads, or on average (75/25) = 3 page reads per query, with a minimum of one page read and a maximum of five page reads when a sequential search is used to solve a query.

The middle section of Figure 6.1 shows an index based on the table. In general terms, an index is any list of keys (column-value + record-address pairs) in order by column value. A DBMS can find a record's address without having to read the table itself by doing a binary search of the index values. So searching for K, L, M, N, or O (the keys in the middle page) takes only one page read, but searching for F, G, H, I, J or P, Q, R, S, T takes two page reads, and searching for A, B, C, D, E or U, V, W, X, Y takes three page reads. (In the last case the DBMS would start with the middle page, go halfway between the middle and the end because the key Y is greater than the key O, and go up again because the key Y is greater than the key T.) That's a total of (5*1) + (5*2) + (5*2) + (5*3) + (5*3) = 55 page reads, or on average (55/25) = 2.2 page reads per query, with a minimum of one page read and a maximum of 3 page reads when a binary search of the index is used to solve a query.

The rightmost section of Figure 6.1 shows an index of the index. This is another ordered list of keys. This time the value of each key is the first key of the index and the record address is the page number of the index. Using this structure, a DBMS searches for A, B, C, D, or E by reading the first page of the index-of-the-index (which points to the first page of the index), and then reading the first index page — a total of two page reads. Searching for F, G, H, I, or J also takes two page reads, as does searching for K, L, M, N, O, for P, Q, R, S, T, and for U, V, W, X, Y. With this structure, all searches take two page reads, never more and never fewer. Not only does a multi-level index require fewer page reads (on average) than a sequential search or a binary index search, it also doesn't gyrate between a minimum and a maximum number of reads. The advantages of a multi-level index are even more pronounced for larger tables. The number of index levels (indexes of the indexes of the indexes ...) can increase indefinitely.

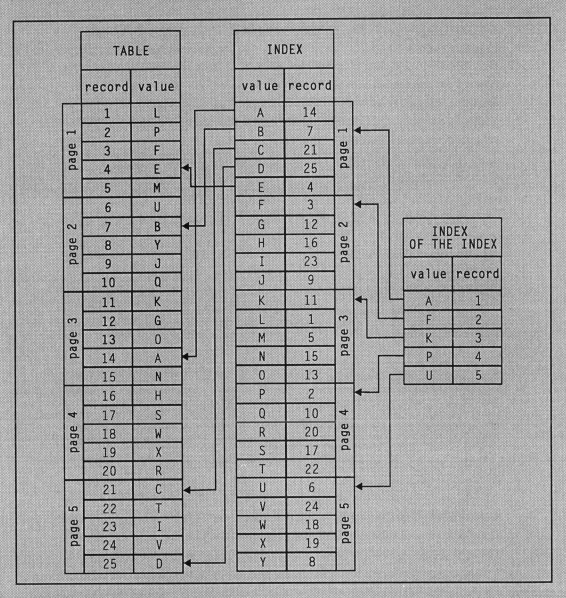

**Figure 6.1**   *A multi-level (B+ tree) index.*

So, if you see frequent *select* statements with a specific column in the *where* clause, you should make sure that column is indexed. And if you see massive UPDATE statements involving the same column, you might want to make sure it's (at least temporarily) not indexed.

# *Checking for Indexes with Embedded SQL*

Because the index status so significantly affects performance, you should always be aware of which columns are indexed. This becomes more difficult as applications become more divorced from databases. A useful addition to every SQL programmer's toolkit is a routine that determines whether a given column is indexed or not. The conventional way to answer the "Is it indexed?" question is to query the database catalog. Because it doesn't acknowledge the existence of indexes, the ANSI SQL standard doesn't provide a way to search for index information in the catalog, but you can write a generic program that will handle most cases.

There are two de facto standards.

The first defacto standard is the one implemented by IBM with its mainframe SQL DBMS product, DB2. A catalog in an IBM DB2 clone has a *SYSINDEXES* table containing information about each index as a whole and a *SYSKEYS* table containing information about each column in the index. The two tables are joinable over the index name, as shown in the following diagram:

| SYSINDEXES | list of indexes | | SYSKEYS | list of columns |
|---|---|---|---|---|
| NAME | index name | <-> | IXNAME | index name |
| TBNAME | base table name | | NAME | column name |
| UNIQUERULE | 'U' if duplicates not allowed | | COLSEQ | column number within index |

The second defacto standard is used by DBMSs with "old style" catalogs. An "old style" catalog will only have a *SYSINDEXES* table containing information about both the index and the index's columns. (Oddly enough, DBMS vendors don't seem to care about the rules of database design, as you can see by their non-normalized catalogs.) If the catalog has no *SYSKEYS* table, the *SYSINDEXES* table is likely to look something like this:

| SYSINDEXES | list of indexes and columns |
|---|---|
| INAME | index name |
| TNAME | base table name |
| INDEXTYPE | 'UNIQUE' if no duplicates allowed |
| COLNAME | column name |
| SEQ | column number within index |

Listing 6.1 is a C function with embedded SQL that queries the catalog for the index status. There is some additional complexity if the program checks for error conditions, if the column can be in a view rather than a base table, or if there can be more than one table/index with the same name but a different owner. You'll find the complete code for this routine on the accompanying diskette, in the file *K_EMBED.C.*

## Listing 6.1

```
    int indexed_column_check ()
    {
    exec sql include sqlca;
    exec sql begin declare section;
        char query_table_name[18+1];
        char query_column_name[18+1];
        int counter;
    exec sql end declare section;
        char ([300];
    printf("Enter table name:"); gets(query_table_name);
    printf("Enter column name:"); gets(query_column_name);

/* First let's settle on what catalog table we actually look up. We could do this
by constructing a command string to be executed dynamically, but it's less complex-
looking if we simply make an appropriate view. */

    exec sql select count(*) into :counter from syskeys;
    if (sqlcode>=0) {       /* if OK, assume DB2-clone catalog type */
        exec sql create view v
        (index_name,table_name,index_type,column_name,column_seq) as
        select i.name,i.tbname,i.uniquerule,k.colname,k.colseq
        from sysindexes i, syskeys k where i.name = k.ixname; }
    else {       /* if not, assume old style catalog type */
        exec sql create view v
        (index_name,table_name,index_type,column_name,column_seq)
        as select iname,tname,indextype,colname,seq
        from sysindexes; }
```

## Listing 6.1 — (continued)

```
/* The simplest query is: Does this column name appear in any of the indexes on
this table name? */

    exec sql select count(*) into :counter from v where column_name =
    :query_column_name and table_name = :query_table_name;
    if (counter==0) return (0);      /* not indexed */
```

/* Yes. The column is used in an index. UPDATEs will slow down whenever this column's value changes. But we don't know much about the effect on SELECTs yet, because if this column is the second or third column in a compound index, then the index isn't in order by this column and usually won't be searched by this column. So add a condition: Is this the index's first column? That is, is its sequence number 1? */

```
    exec sql select count(*) into :counter from v where column_name =
    :query_column_name and table_name = :query_table_name
    and column_seq = 1;
    if (counter==0) return (1);      /* Not first in any index */
```

/* Yes. The column is used in an index, and it's the first in an index. So we would answer the question "Is column X indexed?" with a "yes." But is the column uniquely indexed? Note that it isn't enough to find out that the column is in a UNIQUE index; we should also find out that there is no other column in the same index, i.e., a column with a sequence number of 2. This example won't check for that, though. */

```
    exec sql select count(*) into :counter from v where column_name =
    :query_column_name   and table_name = :query_table_name
    and column_seq = 1 and index_type like 'U%';
    if (counter==0) return (2);      /* not alone in UNIQUE index */
```

/* The column is uniquely indexed. It's safe to throw out the word DISTINCT if you SELECT this column, provided you aren't doing a join. It's likely that this column will be given a high priority in ANDed predicates. (Incidentally, if counter > 1 then there are unnecessary duplicate indexes here.) */

```
    return (3);
    }
```

## *Checking for Indexes with ODBC*

ODBC can answer the "Is the column indexed?" question using the same catalog-query techniques we used with embedded SQL, but there's a better and more standard way — an extended-level-1 ODBC function called *SQLStatistics* which, according to Microsoft's documentation, "retrieves a list of statistics about a single table and the indexes associated with the table. The driver returns the information as a result set." The same document says that "the term table is used for both tables and views, except where the term table or view is used explicitly" — which isn't terribly reassuring, but you should be able to use views or synonyms (i.e., alternate table names) with *SQLStatistics*, as well as base tables.

In essence, *SQLStatistics* acts as if a user input:

```
SELECT <INDEX INFORMATION> FROM <CATALOG TABLES>
WHERE <TABLE NAME = PASSED TABLE NAME>
ORDER BY <INDEX THEN COLUMN>;
```

The result set contains a jumble of information, but we are only concerned with the columns that contain the column name, the column sequence number, the uniqueness test, and the index name. Listing 6.2 is a C function with ODBC that queries the catalog for the index status. Again, this routine is stripped of various error checks and points of detail. The complete code is on the diskette in the file *K_ODBC.C*. (Of course, other complex variations may be appropriate for a particular implementation; one possibility is a timing test to see whether adding or dropping an index affects the execution of a query.)

---

## Listing 6.2

```
#include "sql.h"
#define NON_UNIQUE 4  /*4th in result set, =FALSE if UNIQUE index*/
#define INDEX_NAME 6  /*6th in result set, =name of index */
#define SEQ_IN_INDEX 8/*8th in result set, =col seq no, starts with 1*/
#define COLUMN_NAME 9 /*9th in result set, =name of column*/
```

# Listing 6.2 — continued

```c
int index_column_check (HSTMT hstmt)
{
RETCODE retcode;
char query_table_name[18+1];
SWORD sNonUnique;
UCHAR szIndexName[18+1];
SWORD sSeqInIndex;
UCHAR szColumnName[18+1];
SDWORD cbNonUnique,cbIndexName,cbSeqInIndex,cbColumnName;
int occurs,occursfirst,occursfirstunique;
char query_column_name [18+1];
char uniqueindexname [18+1];
printf("Enter table name:"); gets(query_table_name);
printf("Enter column name:"); gets(query_column_name);

retcode=SQLStatistics(hstmt,NULL,NULL,NULL,NULL,
query_table_name,SQL_NTS,SQL_INDEX_ALL,SQL_QUICK);
if (retcode!=SQL_SUCCESS && retcode!=SQL_SUCCESS_WITH_INFO) {
     return (0); }
SQLBindCol(hstmt,NON_UNIQUE,SQL_C_SHORT,&sNonUnique,0,&cbNonUnique);
SQLBindCol(hstmt,INDEX_NAME,SQL_C_CHAR,szIndexName,18+1,&cbIndexName);
SQLBindCol(hstmt,SEQ_IN_INDEX,SQL_C_SHORT,&sSeqInIndex,0,&cbSeqInIndex);
SQLBindCol(hstmt,COLUMN_NAME,SQL_C_CHAR,szColumnName,18+1,
&cbColumnName);

for (occurs=0,occursfirst=0,occursfirstunique=0;;) {
    retcode=SQLFetch(hstmt);
    if (retcode!=SQL_SUCCESS && retcode!=SQL_SUCCESS_WITH_INFO){
        break; }
    if (stricmp(szColumnName,query_column_name)==0) {
        ++occurs;  /* col occurs in some index */
        if (sSeqInIndex==1) {
            ++occursfirst;    /*col occurs first in some index*/
            if (sNonUnique==FALSE) {
                ++occursfirstunique; /*col occurs first in unique index*/
                strcpy(uniqueindexname,szIndexName); } } }
    else if (sSeqInIndex==2) {
        if (occursfirstunique>0) {
            if (stricmp(uniqueindexname,szIndexName)==0) {
            /* This is the second column of a unique index, for
            which we incremented occursfirstunique. We were
            wrong to do so. */
                --occursfirstunique; } } } }

if (occursfirstunique>0) return (3);/* "column is uniquely indexed"*/
if (occursfirst>0) return (2);      /* "column is indexed"        */
if (occurs>0) return (1);           /* "column is somewhere in index"*/
return (0); }                       /* "column is not in any index"*/
```

# *Optimizing*

Here are four common SQL queries. The queries in Column A do the same thing as the queries in Column B. Which ones will execute faster?

```
COLUMN A                        COLUMN B
SELECT *                        SELECT *
FROM ITEMS                      FROM ITEMS
WHERE PRICE = 600               WHERE .35 = DISCOUNT
AND DISCOUNT = .35;             AND 600 = PRICE;

SELECT *                        SELECT *
FROM INVOICES                   FROM INVOICES
WHERE PD || COUNTRY IN          WHERE PD IN
(SELECT CREDIT || CODE          (SELECT CREDIT
FROM COUNTRY);                  FROM COUNTRY)
                                AND COUNTRY IN
                                (SELECT CODE FROM COUNTRY);


SELECT *                        SELECT *
FROM TABLE_A                    FROM TABLE_A
WHERE COLUMN_A BETWEEN          WHERE COLUMN_A
'a fa' AND 'azfb'               LIKE 'a_fa';
AND COLUMN_A LIKE '__FA';

SELECT *                        SELECT *
FROM COUNTRY                    FROM COUNTRY
WHERE NUM = 5 + 0;              WHERE NUM = 5;
```

The role of the optimizer in the SQL engine is to pick the best path to the answer to a query regardless of the query's syntax. Thus, the optimizer should convert the original syntax of each of these queries to a "canonical form" that reflects the best path. In all of these examples, however, the Column A queries were faster when run against our sample database.

This chapter will show what actually happened when we executed these and other queries, and will explain why, even with the best optimizer, a well-worded query will save money and time. We used three different SQL packages that are commercially available under MS-DOS to run our tests.

The example queries in this chapter show two SQL queries in columns labeled "Query A" and "Query B." In every example, the two queries are logically equivalent and should produce the same result when run against our sample database. Every pair of queries is followed by a timing chart like this one:

```
                Query A        Query B
DBMS #1         100%           200%
DBMS #2         100%           150%
DBMS #3         100%           175%
```

showing the actual execution time for each set of queries as a function of the faster query. (We measured the time elapsed from the pressing of an <EXECUTE> key to the appearance of the last row on the screen and then converted the time in seconds to a base percentage, with the faster time for each pair of responses set at 100%.)

We did it this way because it doesn't matter who made DBMS #1 and it doesn't matter if DBMS #1 is faster than DBMS #2 — this isn't intended to be a DBMS-comparison benchmark. What *does* matter is that Query A is faster than Query B, or at least is no worse. The point of the chart is to demonstrate that one syntax is superior to the other in actual tests with microcomputer database packages.

Following the timing chart, we will try to analyze why one syntax is more efficient. We base our analysis on experience, on the knowledge that sophisticated strategies that work for mainframes don't always work for unsophisticated microcomputer operating systems, on occasional hints found in the reference manuals of products we are familiar with, and on the patterns we see in our own tests.

Bear in mind that every vendor guards its optimizer's secrets. The generalizations that we make in this chapter will not apply to every DBMS in every situation, so you must follow our analyses or recommendations with some skepticism before concluding that they might apply to your application. What we will emphasize, though, is that with more and more support for ODBC, application designers can no longer predict what SQL engine their applications will encounter. In this setting it can only help you to code defensively by optimizing your SQL query syntax.

## OPTIMIZATION RULE-OF-THUMB #1

*If you have two or more ANDed expressions, put the most limiting expression first.*

```
Query A                        Query B

SELECT *                       SELECT *
FROM ITEMS                     FROM ITEMS
WHERE PRICE = 600              WHERE .35 = DISCOUNT
AND DISCOUNT = .35;            AND 600 = PRICE;
```

|          | Query A | Query B |
|----------|---------|---------|
| DBMS #1  | 100%    | 200%    |
| DBMS #2  | 100%    | 200%    |
| DBMS #3  | 100%    | 200%    |

|          | Query A | Query B |
|----------|---------|---------|
| DBMS #1  | 100%    | 100%    |
| DBMS #2  | 100%    | 100%    |
| DBMS #3  | 100%    | 100%    |

The "most limiting" expression is the expression that will return the fewest rows.

In the first timing chart shown above, both *PRICE* and *DISCOUNT* were indexed columns when the queries were run. The second timing chart shows the results of the same queries when only *PRICE* was an indexed column. The *ITEMS* table contains fewer rows where *PRICE=600* than where *DISCOUNT = .35.*

When only the *PRICE* column is indexed, the difference in execution time disappears, but we recommend the Query A syntax regardless (whether or not the columns are indexed). The SQL engine will ignore you if its own evaluation says the Query B syntax is faster, but someday — because an index is added or a table grows — the DBMS may attempt to execute the expressions in the order they appear. If this happens, you'll do better with a command that is already optimized.

Optimizers can use one of two general strategies to execute Query A with the *PRICE = 600* expression first.

### First Strategy: "Driver Index"

```
Loop
{
    Look up first/next entry in index where PRICE = 600, returning ROWID
    If (return from last lookup was 'no more entries in index')
        exit loop
    Read record in Table File for the given ROWID
    If (this record has DISCOUNT = .35)
    {
        Add this ROWID to the list of matches
    }
}
```

### Second Strategy: "List Merge"

```
Loop
{
    Look up first/next entry in index where PRICE = 600, returning ROWID
    If (return from lookup was 'no more entries in index') exit loop
    Add this ROWID to a list of matches
}
If (size of this matchlist is 0) stop
    Loop
    {
        Look up first/next entry in index where DISCOUNT = .35,
        returning ROWID
        If (return from lookup was 'no more entries in index')
            exit loop
        Add this ROWID to a list of matches
    }
```

```
Sort the first list of matches
Sort the second list of matches
Merge the two lists of matches,
    keeping only where ROWIDs are the same
```

If *PRICE* is indexed and *DISCOUNT* is not, an optimizer will always pick the Driver Index strategy with the *PRICE* expression as the driver. Most optimizers will act this way even if the difference is more subtle, e.g.:

☐ if both columns are indexed but one index is *UNIQUE* and the other isn't;

☐ if both *PRICE* and *DISCOUNT* are indexed but one expression uses the "equal to" operator and the other expression uses "greater than or equal to";

☐ if the size of each table is stored in the system catalog, and one table is smaller than the other.

In all of these cases, the optimizer will prefer to use the most limiting expression as the driver, and when it does, the order of the expressions in your SQL statement will not matter. However, our example is not among these cases. For both queries, the optimizer sees two expressions, both using the "equals" operator, on two non-unique indexes for the same table. In such cases, some optimizers will still pick the Driver Index strategy, others will choose a List Merge strategy, and still others will start with one strategy but switch to the other if they reach a threshold number of rows.

While the choice of which expression to start with *could* be random, in practice it isn't. When all other things are equal, optimizers do the first expression in a query first. This is consistent with a general behavior pattern.

The results in the first timing chart look dramatic because we contrived an extreme case: there are no rows at all in the *ITEMS* table in which *PRICE = 600*, and there are 1,008 rows in which *DISCOUNT = .35*. An SQL engine that always uses a List Merge strategy might otherwise be unaffected. However, the chart does show that each DBMS is going through the expressions in the order we gave them, because in either strategy, the query runs slower if *DISCOUNT* is chosen first.

Certainly you can't always know in advance which expression will be the most limiting, but you can probably guess better than your DBMS can.

## OPTIMIZATION RULE-OF-THUMB #2

*Put the table with the smallest number of qualified rows last in the FROM clause and first in the WHERE clause's join expression. Then AND the join expression with a COLUMN >=' ' (an empty string) expression to force the optimizer to choose this expression as the driver.*

```
Query A                    Query B

SELECT *                   SELECT *
FROM INVOICES, COUNTRY     FROM COUNTRY, INVOICES
WHERE                      WHERE
COUNTRY.CODE >= ' '        INVOICES.COUNTRY =
AND COUNTRY.CODE =         COUNTRY.CODE;
INVOICES.COUNTRY;
```

☐ COUNTRY *has 10 rows and* INVOICES *has 4267 rows.*

☐ *Both* COUNTRY.CODE *and* INVOICES.COUNTRY *are indexed columns.*

|         | Query A | Query B |
|---------|---------|---------|
| DBMS #1 | 100%    | 117%    |
| DBMS #2 | 100%    | 167%    |
| DBMS #3 | 100%    | 133%    |

With such a great disparity between the sizes of the tables, it is better to push the DBMS to choose a Driver Index strategy rather than a List Merge strategy if we can. We also want to make sure that it uses COUNTRY.CODE as the driver even if there is some subtle difference between COUNTRY.CODE's index and INVOICE.COUNTRY's index that might incline the optimizer to choose INVOICE.COUNTRY as the driver instead. To get this result, we first ensure that the order of the tables in the FROM clause puts the table with the smallest number of qualified rows last. Then we switch the order of the columns in our join equality expression to COUNTRY.CODE = INVOICES.COUNTRY.

These changes will not affect most optimizers at all, so in addition to switching the expression order, we AND it with COUNTRY.CODE >= ' ' (an empty string). The added expression cannot affect the result, since it's true of all *CHAR* columns that their contents will be *>= ' '* (unless they're *NULL*, but in that case they wouldn't equal the contents of another column anyway).

The optimizer will give a higher priority to the *COLUMN >= ' '* expression than to the *COLUMN = COLUMN* expression because it expects expressions with literals to be more limiting. Thus, the first thing it does is look up *COUNTRY.CODE >= ' '* — this is the driver — and from there it goes on to look up *INVOICES.COUNTRY* only for the 10 rows of *COUNTRY*.

Of course, there is a risk that a rogue optimizer might insist on using a List Merge strategy for a *COLUMN = COLUMN* expression, then merge again with the results of the *COLUMN >= ' '* expression, but that won't affect performance adversely as long as the size of the last table is tiny, as in this example.

## OPTIMIZATION RULE-OF-THUMB #3

*Accuracy before speed. Don't leave off "redundant"* ORDER BY *clauses — they might not be redundant tomorrow.*

```
Query A                    Query B

SELECT *                   SELECT *
FROM INVOICES              FROM INVOICES
WHERE CL# >= 0             WHERE AMOUNT >= 5000
AND AMOUNT >= 5000         ORDER BY CL#;
ORDER BY CL#;
```

☐ *CL# is an indexed column*

☐ *All values of* CL# *are greater than zero.*

|          | Query A | Query B |
|----------|---------|---------|
| DBMS #1  | 100%    | 108%    |
| DBMS #2  | 100%    | 100%    |
| DBMS #3  | 100%    | 112%    |

This is another case where the DBMS has a choice of what order to do things in for Query B. It can:

☐ Retrieve all rows using the index on *CL#*, then remove the rows where *AMOUNT < 5000*. A sort is not necessary because the result was retrieved using the *CL#* index.

☐ Retrieve all rows where *AMOUNT >= 5000*, using a full table scan, then sort the resultant table.

The first choice is better because, in our sample database, *AMOUNT* is not indexed and *AMOUNT >= 5000* returns only a fraction of the rows in the table.

DBMS #1 and DBMS #3 are apparently inclined to take the second, inferior, choice. Query A forces them to take the first choice and use the *CL#* index. This is a full index scan since *CL#* is never *<0*.

The point is, when a DBMS uses a "driver index," in this case *CL#*, the returned rows will be in order by that index. Both DBMS #1 and DBMS #3 do, in fact, return the results of Query A in *CL#* order, so the *ORDER BY CL#* clause is redundant. However, only DBMS #1 realizes it's redundant; DBMS #3 does an extra unnecessary sort, which is interesting because it shows the change in emphasis from dBASE. (Literature about dBASE clones emphasizes that the main purpose of indexes is to support sorts.)

Despite the fact that unnecessary sorts slow things down, we aren't recommending you omit the redundant *ORDER BY* clause in Query A. The second example in this section explains why.

```
Query A                     Query B

SELECT DISTINCT ITEM#       SELECT DISTINCT ITEM#
FROM ITEMS;                 FROM ITEMS ORDER BY ITEM#;
```

☐ *The* ITEMS *table has 6795 rows.*

|         | Query A | Query B |
|---------|---------|---------|
| DBMS #1 | 100%    | 104%    |
| DBMS #2 | 100%    | 100%    |
| DBMS #3 | 100%    | 120%    |

To get the result for these queries, an SQL engine has two choices:

1) Take the first row of the *ITEMS* table and compare the *ITEM#* value to the next 6,794 rows, then take the second row and compare the *ITEM#*

value to the next 6,793 rows, and so on, requiring 6795! (six thousand, seven hundred and ninety-five factorial) accesses.

2) Sort the list (Knuth says that a good sort takes N*log2N n accesses), then go through the sorted list once.

A reasonably good optimizer will check for distinctness by making a sorted list, or by using a pre-sorted list such as an index. In either case, the *ORDER BY* clause becomes unnecessary. However, we can see from the chart that only DBMS #2 was smart enough to figure this out and throw out the *ORDER BY* automatically.

In addition to *DISTINCT* there are three other situations where the result will just "happen" to be in order:

☐ `SELECT X FROM TBL1 GROUP BY X ORDER BY X;`
A *GROUP BY* clause has to use the same procedure as *DISTINCT*. The only difference is that *GROUP BY* is searching for matching values in order to group them, while *DISTINCT* is searching for matching values in order to eliminate them. So *GROUP BY* will also cause the optimizer to make or use a sorted list, for the same reasons given above.

☐ `SELECT X FROM TBL1 WHERE X > 5 ORDER BY X;`
If the optimizer chooses to look up column *X* via an index, the results will be in index order.

☐ `SELECT X FROM TBL1 UNION SELECT Y FROM TBL2 ORDER BY 1;`
The *UNION* operator could really be stated as *UNION DISTINCT*, since *UNION* always gets rid of duplicate rows (unless *UNION ALL* is specified).

Like Odysseus, one can perhaps hear the Sirens calling with the tempting song: "Think of all the time you'll save if you eliminate that redundant clause that does a sort on an already-sorted set." Or, as the matter was once baldly put in an advice column for one SQL DBMS: "if you have a *DISTINCT*, you don't need an *ORDER BY*." The rock the Sirens are standing on is labeled "Not guaranteed that this will be the case in subsequent releases."

If you have the query:

`SELECT DISTINCT X FROM TBL1 ORDER BY X;`

and column *X* has a *unique* index, the optimizer will know that all *X* values are *DISTINCT* by definition. If you leave out the *ORDER BY* clause and the optimizer then leaves out the *DISTINCT* clause, the result won't be what you expect.

## OPTIMIZATION RULE-OF-THUMB #4

*Use a combination of values in a single subquery search, rather than multiple subquery searches.*

Query A

```
SELECT *
FROM INVOICES
WHERE PD || COUNTRY IN
(SELECT CREDIT || CODE
FROM COUNTRY);
```

Query B

```
SELECT *
FROM INVOICES
WHERE PD IN
(SELECT CREDIT
FROM COUNTRY)
AND COUNTRY IN
(SELECT CODE FROM COUNTRY);
```

☐ PD *and* COUNTRY *are one- and three-character columns respectively. Both are indexed.*

|         | Query A | Query B |
|---------|---------|---------|
| DBMS #1 | 100%    | 257%    |
| DBMS #2 | 100%    | 125%    |
| DBMS #3 | 100%    | 121%    |

Query B will do searches on two keys and merge the results.

Query A merges the keys first so it only has to do one search.

The optimizer may not automatically translate Query B into Query A. In the words of Dr. Codd: "DB2's ability to concatenate the name of a city with the name of a state can be used to alter this query into an executable one. However, this is neither a general nor a natural solution to the problem."[1]

You may have seen the following syntax:

```
SELECT * FROM TABLE_A WHERE COLUMN1, COLUMN2 IN
     (SELECT COLUMN1, COLUMN2 FROM TABLE_B);
```

This statement is useful, but it's not part of the ANSI SQL standard syntax. We can come close to it though and stick to ANSI syntax by concatenating *CHAR* fields. Since numbers won't concatenate, you can multiply the first number by an impossibly high value and add the second, for the same effective result with numeric fields.

Note that this advice applies only to subqueries. If the query was:

```
SELECT * FROM TABLE_A WHERE COLUMN1 = 'a' AND COLUMN2 = 'b';
```

then converting to:

```
SELECT * FROM TABLE_A WHERE COLUMN1 || COLUMN2 = 'ab';
```

would not be a good strategy, because if you use any sort of calculation in an expression, the optimizer will choose to do a full table scan, even if there might be an index on either *COLUMN1* or *COLUMN2* or both. In fact, the best way to speed up this search is to make an index with the following:

```
CREATE INDEX <name> ON TABLE_A (COLUMN1,COLUMN2);
```

# OPTIMIZATION RULE-OF-THUMB #5

*Anticipate that* LIKE *won't be optimized after the first* '%' *or* '_'.

Query A

```
SELECT *
FROM TABLE_A
WHERECOLUMN_A BETWEEN
'a fa' AND 'azfb'
AND COLUMN_A LIKE '_ _fa';
```

Query B

```
SELECT *
FROM TABLE_A
WHERE COLUMN_A LIKE 'a_fa';
```

☐ COLUMN_A *is indexed.*

|        | Query A | Query B |
|--------|---------|---------|
| DBMS #1 | 100%   | 200%    |
| DBMS #2 | 100%   | 200%    |
| DBMS #3 | 100%   | 2400%   |

Almost any optimizer will use an index for a *LIKE* expression provided that the first character being searched isn't '_' (the underline character) or '%' (a percent sign). But where will it start and where will it stop? We wanted to see if optimizers would look at every key that began with *a*, filtering out the ones whose third and fourth characters were not *fa*, so our example table has 4000 occurrences of *a*    (less than the minimum possibility) and 4000 occurrences of *azzz* (more than the maximum possibility).

All of the tested DBMSs accelerated when we forced them to start with *a    fa* and stop with *azfb*, as in Query A. This suggests that our conjecture is correct: Query B is going through index keys which are outside the possible range.

The conversion from Query B to Query A is only worthwhile if the number of actual matches is very small compared to the number of keys that begin with the same characters but do not match after the '_' or '%'.

# OPTIMIZATION RULE-OF-THUMB #6

*If your table is small enough to be read in a single disk access, force the optimizer to ignore indexes by adding a "do-nothing" expression.*

Query A

```
SELECT *
FROM COUNTRY
WHERE NUM = 5 + 0;
```

Query B

```
SELECT *
FROM COUNTRY
WHERE NUM = 5;
```

☐ NUM *is an indexed column.*

☐ *All rows of* COUNTRY *can be read in a single disk access.*

|         | Query A | Query B |
|---------|---------|---------|
| DBMS #1 | 100%    | 200%    |
| DBMS #2 | 100%    | 200%    |
| DBMS #3 | 100%    | 100%    |

Query A illustrates how you can force a full table scan even though *NUM* is an indexed column. Of course, you won't often want to! But in this case all the rows in *COUNTRY* can be read in one disk access, while reading the index and then reading the rows would require at least two disk accesses, making a full table scan preferable. (Our tests were done just after booting the computer, so caching has not affected the result.)

DBMS #3's optimizer keeps a "number of rows in the table" statistic in its catalog, which indicates that it's on the lookout for this sort of thing. Other DBMS optimizers simply assume that such a scenario is unlikely, and will always pick an indexed search rather than a full table scan.

However, most optimizers will turn indexing off when faced with an expression, even a do-nothing expression like "add 0," as in this case. The optimizer's expectation is that no expression can be in an index, so it throws in the towel without even bothering to check whether the expression might be exceptionally easy to resolve. The effect is well known and is documented in the database administration manuals of more than one package.

The same effect can be attained for *CHAR* literal values by concatenating them with an empty string (or your DBMS's equivalent). Using a do-nothing scalar function, for example *CHAR('string')*, is less likely to succeed at forcing a scan.

## OPTIMIZATION RULE-OF-THUMB #7

*Use* OR *rather than* UNION *if the predicate columns are unindexed.*

Query A

```
SELECT DISTINCT *
FROM TABLE_A
WHERE COLUMN_C = 5
OR COLUMN_D = 5;
```

Query B

```
SELECT *
FROM TABLE_A
WHERE COLUMN_C = 5
UNION
SELECT *
FROM TABLE_A
WHERE COLUMN_D = 5;
```

☐ COLUMN_C *is not indexed.*

☐ COLUMN_D *is not indexed.*

|        | Query A | Query B |
|--------|---------|---------|
| DBMS #1 | 100%   | 111%    |
| DBMS #2 | 100%   | 105%    |
| DBMS #3 | 100%   | 173%    |

Query B is longer, uses a relatively rare SQL construct, and — in some SQL packages, at least — is illegal as part of a *create view* statement. If Query A always ran faster, as it does in this example, we could recommend that Query B always be converted to Query A. However, this is one case where doing so might actually result in slower execution with some DBMSs (see the example following). To see why, we need to consider two optimizer flaws.

Many optimizers only optimize within a single *WHERE* clause in a single *SELECT* statement. So the two *SELECT*s in Query B are really *both* performed: first the optimizer finds all the rows where COLUMN_C = 5, then it finds all the rows where COLUMN_D = 5 in a separate pass, i.e., it scans the table twice! Therefore, if COLUMN_C is unindexed, Query B should take precisely twice as long to perform as Query A.

If COLUMN_C is indexed, the double search still occurs, but there is an uncommon optimizer flaw, seen in DBMS #2, which more than makes up for this: when this package sees that a predicate contains the word OR, it refuses to use indexes at all; so in this instance, and *only* in this instance with this one package, UNION outperforms OR. (See DBMS #2 in Query A(1) and Query A(2) on rule-of-thumb #8.) Our advice, then, is to use OR rather than UNION if the predicate columns are unindexed.

These observations apply equally well in comparisons of UNION ALL versus OR. If duplicates were permissible, you could replace the queries with:

```
Query A                    Query B

SELECT *                   SELECT *
FROM TABLE_A               FROM TABLE_A
WHERE COLUMN_C = 5         WHERE COLUMN_C = 5
OR COLUMN_D = 5;           UNION ALL
                           SELECT *
                           FROM TABLE_A
                           WHERE COLUMN_D = 5
                           AND COLUMN_C <> 5;
```

Here we've taken the duplicate elimination out of both queries. (In Query A, we did this by removing DISTINCT. In Query B, we did this by replacing UNION with UNION ALL and adding the clause AND COLUMN_C<>5 to the second SELECT so we don't get two rows for every row where both COLUMN_C and COLUMN_D = 5.) Since duplicate elimination is done by sorting, this gets rid of a time-consuming step so both queries will be faster than they were before the change. Query B will still be slower than Query A, though.

## OPTIMIZATION RULE-OF-THUMB #8

*If you have a highly skewed distribution of values in an indexed column, convert a "not equals" expression into a pair of "greater than" and "less than" expressions. If the column is not indexed, always use a "not equals" expression instead.*

Query A(1)

```
SELECT *
FROM INVOICES
WHERE PD > 'Y'
OR PD < 'Y';
```

Query B

```
SELECT *
FROM INVOICES
WHERE PD <> 'Y';
```

*or*

Query A(2)

```
SELECT *
FROM INVOICES
WHERE PD > 'Y'
UNION
SELECT *
FROM INVOICES
WHERE PD < 'Y';
```

☐ *Table* INVOICES *contains 4166 'Y's, 51 'N's, and 50* NULL *values in the* PD *column, which is indexed.*

|  | Query A(1) | Query A(2) | Query B |
|---|---|---|---|
| DBMS #1 | 100% | 100% | 125% |
| DBMS #2 | 400% | 100% | 550% |
| DBMS #3 | 100% | 100% | 200% |

Normally, an optimizer would not know about the preponderance of 'Y' values in the PD column. It would make an assumption (as one package's documentation puts it): "Usually in queries with <>, the number of rows returned is greater than the number of rows skipped ... thus it's usually faster to do a full table scan than use an index."

Since we know that this example isn't the usual case, we split the "not equals" expression into separate "greater than" and "less than" expressions in Query A, knowing that the optimizer is then more likely to use an index. The alternative Query A(2) syntax — using *UNION* instead of *OR* — is discussed in the previous example.

This type of conversion is useful in any query where "not equals" is used with a value that is probably more frequent than all others in an indexed column. When looking for such a situation, remember that:

```
WHERE NOT (A = 5 AND B = 5)
```

is the same as:

```
WHERE A <> 5 OR B <> 5
```

and that:

```
WHERE NOT (A = 5 OR B = 5)
```

is the same as:

```
WHERE A <> 5 AND B <> 5
```

because of a logical rule known as DeMorgan's Law.

The results in this timing chart:

|          | Query A(1) | Query A(2) | Query B |
|----------|------------|------------|---------|
| DBMS #1  | 140%       | 187%       | 100%    |
| DBMS #2  | 300%       | 133%       | 100%    |
| DBMS #3  | 125%       | 200%       | 100%    |

came from running the exact same queries on the same data — except that, this time, the *PD* column was *not* indexed. In this situation, the "not equals" expression is faster.

## OPTIMIZATION RULE-OF-THUMB #9

*Replace the expression* COLUMN IS [NOT] NULL *with* COLUMN >= 'empty string' *for indexed columns. If your DBMS doesn't index* NULLs, *you'll be glad you did. And if it does, you won't have hurt the speed anyway.*

### Corollary #1:
Use *SELECT COUNT(primary-key-column)* rather than *SELECT COUNT(\*)*.

```
Query A                      Query B

SELECT *                     SELECT *
FROM TABLE_A                 FROM TABLE_A
WHERE COLUMN_B >= '  ';       WHERE
                             COLUMN_B IS NOT NULL;
```

☐ COLUMN_B *is indexed.*

|          | Query A | Query B |
|----------|---------|---------|
| DBMS #1  | 100%    | 212%    |
| DBMS #2  | 100%    | 129%    |
| DBMS #3  | 100%    | 100%    |

Since *COLUMN_B*'s data type is *CHAR*, it can't have a value that's less than a blank string. Therefore, Query A returns rows for all cases where *COLUMN_B* has any value at all — except *NULL* — as does Query B.

Everybody knows that *NULLs* have to be represented physically in the database somehow, so you might think the DBMS is simply treating the Query B predicate as:

```
WHERE COLUMN_B NOT = <null value>
```

which would mean that this is just a special case of the advice given for skewed-distribution columns in rule-of-thumb #8. It is. But it is "special" in a subtly interesting manner, having to do with (of all things) optimizing *INSERT*. The command that created the first row in *TABLE_A* was:

```
INSERT INTO TABLE_A (COLUMN_A,COLUMN_B) VALUES ('a',NULL);
```

which is straightforward enough.

But a DBMS designer will look at this and say "Hmmm. I notice that after physically storing *COLUMN_B* in the table file, I have to construct a key based on the 'value' *NULL* and add that to the index. That means I have to: (a) look up the index value to establish its position in the index file, which probably requires several disk accesses and still more time for inserting the new value and rewriting at least one index page, and (b) allow more space in the index file. Why am I going to all that bother? Users put *NULLs* in because they'll figure out the true value later or the information doesn't apply — they *don't care*. There's no query expression that can ever be true for *NULLs*, except *IS [NOT] NULL*. So, in a non-unique index, I just won't add *NULL* keys."

Both DBMS #1 and DBMS #2, as well as some others we know of, appear to have chosen this path, and as a result, their *INSERT* and *UPDATE* operations are faster, and they use less storage space as an added bonus. On the other hand, such DBMSs are forced to do full table scans when confronted by the *IS NULL* or *IS NOT NULL* operators. Incidentally, these DBMSs also cannot use an index for *COUNT(*)*, the only aggregate function that notices *NULLs*, so with these systems it might be better to: *SELECT COUNT(primary-key-column)* rather than *SELECT COUNT(*)*.

# OPTIMIZATION RULE-OF-THUMB #10

*Avoid Cartesian products on tables with large numbers of rows. Create a temporary table and index and use that in your query instead.*

Query A

```
CREATE TABLE TMP
(COL1 INT);

INSERT INTO TMP
SELECT (NUM + AMOUNT)*2
FROM COUNTRY, INVOICES;

CREATE INDEX I ON TMP (COL1);

SELECT PRICE
FROM TMP, ITEMS
WHERE COL1 = PRICE;

DROP TABLE TMP;
```

Query B

```
SELECT PRICE
FROM COUNTRY, INVOICES, ITEMS
WHERE NUM + AMOUNT =
PRICE / 2;
```

|          | Query A | Query B |
|----------|---------|---------|
| DBMS #1  | 100%    | 2500%+  |
| DBMS #2  | 100%    | 2500%+  |
| DBMS #3  | 100%    | 2500%+  |

Nuclear engineers talk of reactor masses that have "gone critical." DBMS designers talk of joins that have "gone Cartesian." A Cartesian product is the join of everything in one table with everything in a second table. For example, given two tables *T1* and *T2*:

| T1 |
|----|
| 1 |
| 2 |

| T2 |
|----|
| 1 |
| 2 |

The Cartesian product is:

| T1.COLUMN | T2.COLUMN |
|-----------|-----------|
| 1 | 1 |
| 1 | 2 |
| 2 | 1 |
| 2 | 2 |

A Cartesian product always contains the number of rows in table *T1* multiplied by the number of rows in table *T2*. In our example, there are 10 rows in COUNTRY, 4,267 rows in INVOICES, and 6,795 rows in ITEMS. Thus, the number of rows in the Cartesian product is 289,942,650 — which takes a *long* time to search, as shown by the timing results for Query B.

We acknowledge that Query A is less clear than Query B because only an expert would understand why we're making a temporary table and index. We acknowledge that Query A is less portable than Query B because you can't fit this *query* A into a view and because not every user will have the privilege to create tables and indexes. But when you see funny-looking joins like the one in Query B, you can expect some DBMS's reactors to go Cartesian — which is definitely something to avoid.

The definition of "funny-looking joins" is: joins where the expressions contain calculations, joins where the expressions are un-indexed on both sides, and joins that contain no expressions at all. Users shouldn't be permitted to do funny-looking joins ad hoc, which means the responsibility of anticipating and preparing for them is up to you. Temporary tables and indexes, as in Query A, are a feasible option.

Keep in mind that this tip works only if the Cartesian product is really large. Up to a certain point, the per-call overhead of Query A will obviously use up more time than going Cartesian on a join will. Doing a few sample queries with your DBMS should allow you to pinpoint when rule-of-thumb #10 becomes applicable.

## OPTIMIZATION RULE-OF-THUMB #11

*Use* >= MAX(COLUMN) *rather than* >= ALL COLUMN.

Query A

```
SELECT AMOUNT
FROM INVOICES
WHERE AMOUNT >=
(SELECT MAX(PRICE)
FROM ITEMS);
```

Query B

```
SELECT AMOUNT
FROM INVOICES
WHERE AMOUNT >= ALL
(SELECT PRICE FROM ITEMS);
```

|         | Query A | Query B |
|---------|---------|---------|
| DBMS #1 | 100%    | 124%    |
| DBMS #2 | 100%    | 600%    |
| DBMS #3 | 100%    | 2700%   |

The sort of query we're trying to answer here, expressed in English, is "What values in *INVOICES.AMOUNT* are larger than the largest value in *ITEMS.PRICE?*"

Amazing but true: in ANSI SQL, Query A and Query B are not precisely equivalent, unless *ITEMS.PRICE* is de facto a *NOT NULL* column.

If a table *T* has one row containing *COLUMN = 1* and one row containing *COLUMN = NULL*, i.e.:

| T |
|---|
| 1 |
| ? |

then a search for *MAX(COLUMN)* returns 1, because the *MAX* scalar function ignores *NULL*s. But a search for *COLUMN >= ALL...* does not ignore *NULL*s, and since there is no value that is >= *NULL*, such a search will return nothing. Some SQL packages simply ignore this rule, but we used a *NOT NULL* column in our tests to avoid confusion.

Our representative SQL packages all do a relatively good job with Query A, especially because *PRICE* is an indexed column. If we drop the index, all of them slow down somewhat, but are still able to do Query A faster than they do Query B *with* the index. Perhaps the vendors have paid less attention to >= *ALL* because authorities on SQL usage have recommended that it should be avoided.

## OPTIMIZATION RULE-OF-THUMB #12

*Use the Law of Transitivity when writing* WHERE *clauses.*

Query A

```
SELECT
INVOICES.INV#,
ITEMS.ITEM#
FROM INVOICES, ITEMS
WHERE
INVOICES.INV# = '1209-92'
AND ITEMS.INV# = '1209-92';
```

Query B

```
SELECT
INVOICES.INV#,
ITEMS.ITEM#
FROM INVOICES, ITEMS
WHERE INVOICES.INV# =
ITEMS.INV# AND
INVOICES.INV# = '1209-92';
```

☐ *Both* INVOICES.INV# *and* ITEMS.INV# *are indexed.*

|          | Query A | Query B |
|----------|---------|---------|
| DBMS #1  | 100%    | 100%    |
| DBMS #2  | 100%    | 150%    |
| DBMS #3  | 100%    | 464%    |

The Law of Transitivity states:

If A = B and B = C, then A = C

If you look at Query B, you will notice that *INVOICES.ITEM* must equal *1209-92*. From this, you can see that the expression *INVOICES.INV# = ITEMS.INV#* can be replaced with the expression *'1209-92' = ITEMS.INV#*, and that is what we did to translate Query B to the more efficient Query A.

Query A is more efficient because it's easier to look up the two indexed values and merge the results than to look up the one value of *INVOICES.INV#* in the index, retrieve the actual row from the tablespace, construct a key based on *INVOICES.INV#*, then look up *ITEMS.INV#* in the index based on that key value.

As usual, there are some database packages that will do this conversion automatically, but there are also some that won't.

When it's a question of replacing a column name with a literal value, as above, the Query A syntax is always preferable. Less common, and more doubtful, is the case of replacing one column name with another, e.g.:

```
Query A                          Query B

SELECT *                         SELECT *
FROM A, B, C                     FROM A, B, C
WHERE                            WHERE
A.COLUMN = B.COLUMN AND          A.COLUMN = B.COLUMN AND
A.COLUMN = C.COLUMN;             B.COLUMN = C.COLUMN;
```

Here the question is strictly "Which of the two columns, *A.COLUMN* or *B.COLUMN*, is more easily searched given all indexing considerations?" Pick the one that's defined as *UNIQUE* or as the *PRIMARY KEY*.

The Law of Transitivity also extends to:

```
If A > B and B > C then A > C
If A < B and B <= C then A <= C
```

and so on.

Watch for traps though — both of the following statements are false because A might equal C:

```
If A > B and B >= C then A > C
If A <> B and B <> C then A <> C
```

## OPTIMIZATION RULE-OF-THUMB #13

*OR should not be used to enumerate a long series. And, since IN is always converted to OR it shouldn't be used either. Use BETWEEN instead.*

Query A

```
SELECT *
FROM INVOICES
WHERE CL#
BETWEEN 20 AND 25
AND CL# <> 23;
```

Query B(1)

```
SELECT *
FROM INVOICES
WHERE CL# = 20
OR CL# = 21
OR CL# = 22
OR CL# = 24
OR CL# = 25;
```

*or*

Query B(2)

```
SELECT *
FROM INVOICES
WHERE CL#
IN(20, 21, 22, 24, 25);
```

☐ *CL# is an indexed column.*

|         | Query A | Query B |
|---------|---------|---------|
| DBMS #1 | 100%    | 260%    |
| DBMS #2 | 100%    | 125%    |
| DBMS #3 | 100%    | 275%    |

Query A is better than Query B if *CL#*'s data type is *SMALLINT* or *INTEGER*, as in our example. The number of expressions is less, and the possibility that an index will be used for the search is higher.

One thing that all SQL DBMS packages can be relied on to do is change *IN* to *OR*. With all the packages we tested, both of the alternate Query B syntaxes took precisely the same length of time.

This brings up a point that puzzles us. We read the following statement in an SQL advice column recently:

"Avoid using modifiers such as *IN, BETWEEN, LIKE, NOT,* and *OR,* as these usually result in complete table scans of the table being examined. ... You can easily convert *BETWEEN* clauses into range comparisons ..."[2]

Since our gut feeling was that the optimizer usually does *not* do a complete table scan in such cases, we ran each of the following queries twice with our three DBMSs to test this assumption:

```
Query A                        Query B

SELECT *                       SELECT *
FROM INVOICES                  FROM INVOICES
WHERE CL#                      WHERE CL# >= 20
BETWEEN 20 AND 25;             AND CL# <= 25;
```

The following timing chart shows the result when *CL#* is an indexed column:

|         | Query A | Query B |
|---------|---------|---------|
| DBMS #1 | 100%    | 100%    |
| DBMS #2 | 100%    | 100%    |
| DBMS #3 | 100%    | 100%    |

The following timing chart shows the result of the same two queries after the index on *CL#* has been dropped:

|         | Query A | Query B |
|---------|---------|---------|
| DBMS #1 | 100%    | 100%    |
| DBMS #2 | 100%    | 100%    |
| DBMS #3 | 100%    | 100%    |

*BETWEEN* performed just as well as the range comparisons in our tests. Although the indexed searches ran much faster than the un-indexed searches, in both cases all three of our DBMSs took the same amount of time to process Query A as they did to process Query B.

## OPTIMIZATION RULE-OF-THUMB #14

*If neither the outer* SELECT, *nor the simple* IN *sub-*SELECT *of a query can return a duplicate value, and the selection isn't part of a possibly-updatable view or cursor, replace the subquery with a join. If there is a* DISTINCT *in the query or the query isn't likely to be harmed by adding* DISTINCT, *replace the subquery with a join and add* DISTINCT. *(Note: this rule does not apply for certain minor exceptions; see below.)*

```
Query A                          Query B



SELECT DISTINCT                  SELECT DISTINCT INV#
INVOICES.INV#                    FROM INVOICES
FROM INVOICES, ITEMS             WHERE
WHERE                            INV# IN
INVOICES.INV# = ITEMS.INV#;      (SELECT INV# FROM ITEMS);
```

|          | Query A | Query B |
|----------|---------|---------|
| DBMS #1  | 100%    | 395%    |
| DBMS #2  | 100%    | 476%    |
| DBMS #3  | 100%    | 108%    |

"The difference in performance of nested and non-nested versions of the same query puts an unnecessary performance-oriented burden on users, which will not disappear until nesting is prohibited or the translatability problem is completely solved and incorporated into DBMS optimizers. In nested queries, as in non-nested ones, duplicate rows must be prohibited to avoid the additional burden of unexpected discrepancies in the results." — E.F.Codd, "Fatal Flaws in SQL," *Datamation*, August 15, 1988

"IBM has been telling us for years that joins are generally more efficient than subselects." — *Database Programming & Design Magazine*, December 1990

"Whenever possible, try to use joins instead of nested or correlated queries." — documentation for a well-known SQL product

"Don't use joins when you can use subqueries." — newsletter for another well-known SQL product

Ever wonder what the word "structured" stands for in "Structured Query Language?" The story is that the early designers wanted to present a syntax that looked less complex than joins. The syntax:

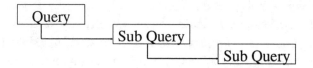

is the structure they wanted to emphasize as SQL's unique selling feature, the construct that distinguished it from other, proposed, non-hierarchical database languages. Ironically though, the one thing everyone seems to agree on is that you should avoid what SQL was originally all about, namely subqueries.

The recommended process is called "flattening," because we're taking the multiple-level subquery statement and changing it to a single-level join statement. "Flattening" is what this example shows (Query B is unflattened; Query A is the flattened equivalent). Query A runs faster than Query B. It looks nicer, too.

Given that joins are better than subqueries, we now face the questions:

□ Why don't the DBMS vendors convert automatically?

□ Precisely how does one convert subqueries to joins?

Why *don't* DBMS vendors simply translate all subquery-based selections into join-based selections? Possibly because:

□ Views with selections based on joins are often considered non-updatable, even if the columns of only one table are actually selected.

□ If the sub-*SELECT* can return duplicate values, unwanted duplications could appear in the result. Consider what would happen if *TABLE_A* contained the values *{1,2}* in *COLUMN_A*, and *TABLE_B* contained the values *{1,1}* in *COLUMN_A*. Then, for the following queries:

Query A

```
SELECT A.COLUMN_A
FROM TABLE_A A, TABLE_B B
WHERE A.COLUMN_A = B.COLUMN_A;
```

Query B

```
SELECT A.COLUMN_A
FROM TABLE_A
WHERE A.COLUMN_A IN
  (SELECT COLUMN_A FROM TABLE_B);
```

Query A would return:

| COLUMN_A |
|----------|
| 1 |
| 1 |

Query B, on the other hand, would return:

| COLUMN_A |
|----------|
| 1 |

There is no way to make a join which is a simple flattening of Query B, and which returns the same answer, because of the duplicate values in the columns, so DBMS vendors don't normally try. However, you can get around this in two different ways.

The first solution: check whether the column *B.COLUMN_A* is *UNIQUE*. If it is, unwanted duplications can't happen, so the next step isn't necessary. If it isn't, then eliminate all duplicates from the result by using *SELECT DISTINCT*.

Unfortunately, this will also eliminate any duplicates that are correctly present in the original (subquery) search, so you'll also have to check whether the column *A.COLUMN_A* is *UNIQUE*. If it is, the only duplications that *DISTINCT* will remove are from *B.COLUMN_A*, so there's no loss of information.

*DISTINCT* is expensive (it usually involves a sort), but even so, it often works out better than using a subquery without a *DISTINCT*.

The second solution: simply ignore the problem and declare that *{1,1}* is the right answer for Query B! We aren't recommending this solution, but must include it for completeness because it might be forced on you automatically by an optimizer. There's a popular "ANSI SQL textbook" that illustrates subqueries coming out with such results and calls them the right answer although the DBMS they are actually describing has been criticized for such behavior. Apparently the DBMS in question is always flattening subqueries even if the results are bizarre.

At the other extreme from this "always flatten" product is another that never flattens. In the middle are products that sometimes flatten if they calculate that unwanted duplication couldn't happen. But there is some possibility that the calculation could get too complex.

There are also some exceptional situations where the subquery is faster, so consult the product liturature of your own DBMS. We are advised that, in the case of one SQL engine, Query B is faster when the subquery will return only one value. In another product, the subquery works better if neither *TABLE_A.COLUMN_A* nor *TABLE_B.COLUMN_A* are indexed.

Rule-of-thumb #14 applies to non-*IN* subqueries too, although the methods get trickier. Consider a subquery following *> ANY*:

```
SELECT DISTINCT COLUMN_A FROM TABLE_A
WHERE COLUMN_A > ANY (SELECT COLUMN_A FROM TABLE_B);
```

This can be replaced with:

```
SELECT DISTINCT TABLE_A.COLUMN_A FROM TABLE_A, TABLE_B
GROUP BY TABLE_A.COLUMN_A
HAVING MAX (SELECT COLUMN_A FROM TABLE_B);
```

These statements are not precisely equivalent because of some obscure rules about *NULL*s, discussed in Chapter 2, but the rules are often ignored in any case.

## OPTIMIZATION RULE-OF-THUMB #15

*Unless you know for a fact that your DBMS has special optimization routines for* EXISTS, *use* IN. *If you're porting code from an old SQL DBMS application, be suspicious when you see correlated subqueries. The code might have been written for a specific DBMS and may perform poorly in other packages.*

```
Query A                              Query B

SELECT *                             SELECT *
FROM ITEMS                           FROM ITEMS
WHERE INV# IN                        WHERE EXISTS
(SELECT INV# FROM INVOICES           (SELECT * FROM INVOICES
WHERE CL# < 75);                     WHERE INVOICES.INV# =
                                     ITEMS.INV# AND CL# < 75);
```

☐ *Both* INVOICES.INV# *and* ITEMS.INV# *are indexed.* CL# *is not.*

|         | Query A | Query B |
|---------|---------|---------|
| DBMS #1 | 100%    | 248%    |
| DBMS #2 | 100%    | 188%    |
| DBMS #3 | 225%    | 100%    |

This example shows that sometimes which DBMS you are using matters a great deal. However, our experience is that DBMS #3 is an exception in the DBMS world — it appears that the majority of vendors cannot automatically optimize *EXISTS*.

A very good optimizer might take the two indexes, which are sorted lists, and merge them to produce a quick result — as quick as if the queries were joins. The chart would not show any difference between Query A and Query B because the same process was followed for both.

Good strategy: An optimizer can handle Query A by doing the inner *SELECT* first. Remember that the result of any *SELECT* is a table, at least a virtual one, and we'll call this result table *T*. Now the optimizer can create a temporary index:

```
CREATE INDEX TMP ON T (INV#);
```

Then it can do a full table scan on *ITEMS*, making a key from the *INV#* value in each row and looking it up in the *TMP* index. Each time there's a match, the optimizer adds *ITEM*'s ROWID to the final result set. (A variant scenario: some database packages would sort all the rows in table *T* and all the rows in table *ITEMS*, then merge the two sorted lists.)

Poor strategy: The optimizer can handle Query A by doing the outer *SELECT* first. Again, the result is a (virtual) table *T*, and again a temporary index is created. Next, a full table scan on *INVOICES* is done, making a key from the *INV#* value in each row and looking it up in the *TMP* index. Each time there's a match, the optimizer adds both *ITEMS*'s ROWID and *INVOICES*'s ROWID to a temporary result set. Then the optimizer goes through the temporary result set, eliminating rows where *INVOICES.CL# > 75* and projecting so that only *ITEMS*' s ROWID remains. Lastly, *ITEMS*' s ROWID is sorted so that duplicates can be eliminated.

Why is the second strategy poor? Because the optimizer is going from the outer *SELECT* to the inner *SELECT*, the result is in order by item's columns, which means that the DBMS will be adding redundant rows and having to get rid of them later. Worse: the join (which expands the size of the result set) takes place before the < *75* expression is evaluated (which limits the size of the result set).

Correlated subqueries have to be done from the outermost to the innermost query. If the optimizer doesn't realize it can convert Query B to Query A automatically, there is a high risk it will pick the poor strategy.

One DBMS vendor's manual recommends the correlated subquery be used "if the correlated field is indexed and the nested query returns a large amount of data."

## OPTIMIZATION RULE-OF-THUMB #16

*Don't trust an SQL package to optimize away a repetitive calculation. Do it yourself to be sure. You can always add a comment.*

```
Query A                    Query B

SELECT *                   SELECT *
FROM TABLE_B               FROM TABLE_B
WHERE COL1 = 2;            WHERE COL1 = 200000 / 100000;
```

☐ TABLE_B *has 10,000 rows.*

☐ COL1 *is unindexed.*

|         | Query A | Query B |
|---------|---------|---------|
| DBMS #1 | 100%    | 108%    |
| DBMS #2 | 100%    | 227%    |
| DBMS #3 | 100%    | 225%    |

Because *COL1* is unindexed, the DBMS does a full table scan.

What we were trying to find out was: When does the optimizer do the calculation *200000 / 100000*? If it does it once for all at the start, then the effect is negligible and Query B will take the same time as Query A. If it does the division *every time it looks at a row*, then Query B will run slower. Query B runs slower on all three packages, so it appears the DBMSs (especially DBMS #2 and DBMS #3) do not optimize the repetitive calculation.

### An additional note on arithmetic:

Often, numbers in database files are stored in ASCII or BCD, not binary. To some extent, this is because numeric storage formats are not as portable. Another factor is the influence of dBASE. (Some SQL packages can use dBASE-format .*DBF* files directly as the physical representation of table data, which means the underlying storage is exclusively in ASCII.)

If the storage is non-binary, then the basic arithmetic package ought to be non-binary too. For instance, it's inefficient to load two ASCII numbers, then convert them to binary, then add them together, when one can just use ASCII arithmetic to add them.

But will the makers of such packages also have good routines for binary or floating-point arithmetic? Their efforts in this direction can be expected to be commensurate with the amount of demand from their users. Which is to say, none. (When did you ever see a review of an SQL package that benchmarked the speed of arithmetic in scalar functions or expressions?) The suspicion, then, is that even simple integer arithmetic is slower in SQL than in the SQL host language, such as C, and this suspicion *was* shown to be correct for the only package we were able to test.

Of course, moving a function to the host language "because it's faster" is not a good idea if there is an offsetting loss, such as a less readable or less portable program. In most cases, however, it would probably be better to have your host compiler, rather than your SQL engine, do arithmetic routines.

## OPTIMIZATION RULE-OF-THUMB #17

*If you have two or more ORed expressions, put the least limiting expression first.*

Query A

```
SELECT COUNT(*)
FROM TABLE_A
WHERE X = 0 OR Y = 0;
```

Query B

```
SELECT COUNT(*)
FROM TABLE_A
WHERE Y = 0 OR X = 0;
```

☐ Both X and Y are unindexed columns.

☐ Column X always contains 0; column Y always contains 1.

|          | Query A | Query B |
|----------|---------|---------|
| DBMS #1  | 100%    | 162%    |
| DBMS #2  | 100%    | 100%    |
| DBMS #3  | 100%    | 102%    |

The "least limiting" expression is the expression which will return the most rows.

Rule-of-thumb #1 says if you have two or more *AND*ed expressions, put the most limiting expression first. This rule for two *OR*ed expressions advises the reverse: put the *less* limiting expression first.

Logic says if the expression *X = 0* is *TRUE*, then the expression *X = 0 OR Y = 0* is also *TRUE*. We can illustrate this logic with a C program that prints *Y = 1*, proof that it never tries to evaluate the expression *(Y=0)==0*:

```
void main ()
{
    int    x,y=1;
    if ((x=0)==0||(y=0)==0);
    printf("y=%d\n",y);
}
```

If the DBMS evaluates *X = 0* first (a condition which is always *TRUE* in our test database) it won't need to evaluate *Y = 0*. But if the DBMS evaluates *Y = 0* first (a condition which is always *FALSE* in our test database) it must proceed to calculate *X = 0* too. So, if the optimizer evaluates the expressions in the order given in Query A, it can get by with one evaluation per row. But if it evaluates the expressions in the order given by Query B, it has to do two evaluations.

The logic applies only to a DBMS which makes a single pass through all the rows when it solves a simple pair of unindexed *OR*ed conditions. DBMS #1 must be such a DBMS. It runs Query A much faster then Query B and proves the rule. DBMS #2 is not such a DBMS. It does two passes and *UNION*s the results (as we saw in the timing chart for rule-of-thumb #7), so Query A and Query B take the same amount of time. DMBS #3 runs Query A only slightly faster than Query B; perhaps it can evaluate *Y = 0* so quickly that the effect is barely measurable.

If it's impossible to guess which of two expressions is more likely to be *TRUE*, put the less complex one first. For instance use:

```
X=0 OR (X*X/5)/1.1 > Y
```

rather than

```
(X*X/5)/1.1 > Y OR X = 0
```

in the hope that the DBMS will sometimes find that the simple expression is *TRUE* and therefore will skip the complex expression.

# *Summary*

SQL offloads "choosing the best query path" questions from the back of the application designer and dumps them on the DBMS vendor. The problem is: not all SQL packages do this very well in all cases.

The results we have seen are bad news. They show that if you construct a query "the right way," you can make it go faster, even though the choice of syntax should not matter. On the other hand, Column A queries are always better than Column B queries, or at least they're rarely worse. So if you learn "the right way" for vendor 1, it's probably not "the wrong way" for vendor 2. This consistency occurs because the underlying fundamental technology is often the same; the basics of SQL are well known to all vendors.

Of course, SQL packages are always improving. It would not be surprising if, by the time you read this, all of the packages we tested are sporting new optimizers which can automatically handle many of the optimizations we recommend. And if you switch to a more advanced microcomputer operating system with multi-threading, such as IBM's OS/2 and Microsoft's Windows NT, you are likely to encounter a much more sophisticated breed of DBMS, because many of the cleverest optimizations require multi-threading.

We think, though, that such advances will not obsolete our recommendations because — also by the time you read this — untried new packages will be introduced on the market with completely unsophisticated optimizers. If you don't know what package your program will encounter, it's best to be safe and rely on the rules-of-thumb. When formulating those rules, we took a sampling of optimizers at various levels of development and analyzed their shortcomings with — we hope — sufficient thoroughness to prepare you for the shortcomings you'll be encountering in the years to come.

# *References*

1. E.F. Codd "Fatal Flaws in SQL," *Datamation*, August 15, 1988.

2. "Client-Side Performance Tuning," *DBMS Magazine*, November 1993.

# *Beneath the Covers*

What's the connection between a base table and an MS-DOS file?

What do indexes look like on the hard disk?

Are all commercial SQL implementations written in C? No. But high-level languages are written in low-level languages, generally C or assembler. Thus, when we see an *UPDATE* statement, it's legitimate to think of an SQL engine using disk I/O functions similar to those found in the standard C library to process it (*fopen()* to open a file, *lseek()* to position at the right record location, *fread()* to get the current contents of the record, *fwrite()* to write the new contents, *fclose()* to close the file) — something similar to this has to be happening, but what?

Are such questions any of our business?

We don't really know the answers to these questions, except for the last one — we're going to *make* it our business. We know that ordinary disk files are being read and written with unmagical means, we know that most SQL vendors are hiding the details, and in this chapter, we're going to explore what we think must be inside their black boxes.

## How Data is Stored

The most primitive table/file relationship imaginable is the *.DBF* file. The *.DBF* file is a near-standard way of storing data used by Borland International, Inc.'s dBASE, its numerous clones, and many other programs. A *.DBF* file can store only a single "table." A header at the start of the file contains basic information about the file and a list of the "columns" in the "table" as follows:

| Structure | Comment |
|---|---|
| File Header | occurs once |
| Field Headers | occur once per "column" |
| Data Records | occur once per "record" |

This structure is fixed. There are only a few variations and only a few ways to store data. The *ODBF_DOS.C* programming example in Chapter 5 includes a fairly thorough description of *.DBF* files, so we'll skip the details here.

Because the *.DBF* format is so widely used and so easily understood, it is invaluable for import/export routines. This is true not only for transferring data between DBMS packages, but also for moving data from the DBMS to a commercial reporting program (such as Crystal or R+R).

Historically, though, the *.DBF* isn't just an import/export adjunct. It is an actual database foundation. There are some apparent advantages to storing the database as *.DBF* files:

☐ An error in a *.DBF* file is easily patched. A programmer who knows the file structure can either write a patch program or use one of the packages available commercially (such as dSalvage or the Norton Utilities).

☐ The storage is fixed, so it's easy to predict how much space you need in advance. And you can be confident the ROWID never changes.

Nevertheless, the *.DBF* format is the basis for only a few SQL systems. Some of the problems that have caused this trend away from *.DBFs* could perhaps be solved by definitional changes. For example:

☐ The 10-byte restriction on field name size is less than the ANSI SQL standard requirement.

☐ There is no standard way to store *NULLs*.

☐ There is no variable-character support. (It is possible to store data in a separate *memo* file, but there's no agreement on what a *memo* file looks like.)

☐ The header size and record size are both fixed, so the SQL statement "*alter table ... add <new column>...*" results in a remake of the entire file.

☐ The data is, in fact, too easy to get at. What's the point of having a fancy *grant/revoke* privilege granting system if anybody can simply use a patch program to change the database?

But the real reason for the trend away from *.DBF*s is that simple "one-file-one-table, one- table-one-file" structures can't handle the complex interplay of data, indexes, and code that is becoming commonplace.

## *Classic and Radical Structures*

Figure 8.1 shows the classic, or Portuguese man-o'war, database structure which is still the fundamental starting point of most SQL databases.

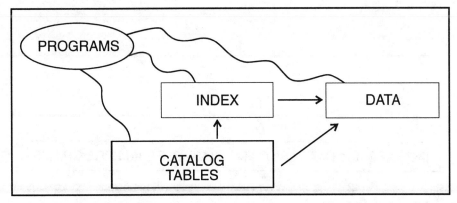

**Figure 8.1**     *The classic, or Portuguese man-o' war database structure.*

Figure 8.2 shows the radical database structure.

Figure 8.2 isn't trying to suggest that the radical structure is in fact not structured. On the contrary: database *management* implies database *organization*. In the radical structure, the different types of data are still separated, but they are not separated in space. They're stored contiguously but kept separate logically.

In a classic database structure, the "types" of data are separated at the file level (indexes are in different files from tables, etc.). In a radical database structure, the separation is done by markings or program logic within a page or a file or some other logical unit.

For example, consider the effect of these two SQL statements:

```
CREATE TABLE T
     (S1 INT NOT NULL PRIMARY KEY,
     S2 CHAR(5) CHARACTER SET ANSI);

INSERT INTO T VALUES (100,'C');
```

In a conventional classic database, we would end up with three files:

| Catalog | Table | Primary Key Index |
|---------|-------|-------------------|
| T | 0000100 | 0000100 |
| S1 | C.... ⇐ | pointer to record #0 |
| S2 | | |

INDEXES and DATA and CATALOG-TABLES and PROGRAMS

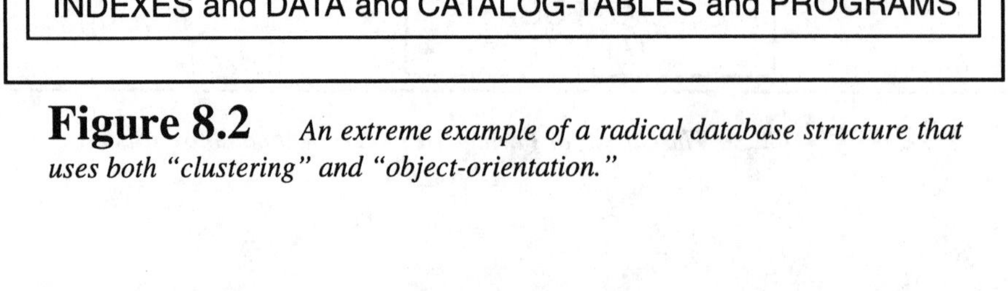

**Figure 8.2**  *An extreme example of a radical database structure that uses both "clustering" and "object-orientation."*

Here is an example of the same entries in a radical database:

| Catalog + Table + Primary Key Index Etc. |
|---|
| "main description of T" = "S1 INT NOT NULL,S2 CHAR(5)" |
| .................................................................................. |
| "domain description" = "S2 CHAR(5) CHARACTER SET ANSI" |
| "primary key value" = 0000100 |
| "related file" = <none> |
| "no further data" |
| "code" = "if (time-of-day > 17:00) then primary-key-value = 0" |

In this structure:

☐ *domain description* shows that this item, for instance, was inserted with the specified character set in force.

☐ *primary key value* shows the value of the inserted primary key. The rows in table *T* are physically sorted ("clustered") by the primary key values; that is, the data file is structured in a B-tree, just like a classic index. The difference is that instead of being followed by a pointer to the data record (as in an index) the key value is followed immediately by the data itself. The advantage is obvious: when you look up the primary key, there is no extra disk I/O to read the record itself. The disadvantage is that the physical address (ROWID) is volatile because new rows can be inserted earlier on the same page or the page can split. Therefore, secondary-key indexes can't point directly to the physical address, and access by secondary key is slow.

☐ *related file* shows a pointer to another file (in this case, there is none). Sometimes special data won't fit in the main file — for instance, binary representations of photographs. Such data, called a BLOB (Binary Large OBject) usually gets a file of its own.

☐ *no further data* shows that there is no further related *physical* data. The DBMS knows that if there is nothing here, then it must use the value defined in the `CREATE TABLE DEFAULT` clause — space is saved on the theory that often the value will equal the defined default.

☐ *code* shows a related piece of code. This can be a "method" or a "trigger." It can be binary but is more likely in a high-level language. Again, it may merely be a pointer — it depends on whether the code applies only to this value or to the table as a whole (in which case, the method would be here only if this is a catalog).

For competitive reasons, most serious DBMS packages will have to incorporate at least some of the non-conventional structure exemplified here — there are potential performance advantages in terms of space, number of disk accesses, and flexibility. Also, maintenance should theoretically become easier with OOP techniques. The disadvantage is that the structure will be too complicated, and perhaps too secret, to manipulate with low level code — programmers will have to use the database routines. And obviously, since each vendor will have his own ideas, the structure will be "proprietary," meaning "every vendor will have his own." Forget about standardizing around a file format as was possible in the Deebeehefozooic Era; the only real standard will be the language. (Note: this prediction could be wrong if a flexible one-file-for-all structure, such as the one in Microsoft Access, is adopted as a starting point by other vendors.)

## *Saving Space in Data Files*

Because SQL deliberately hides the details of data file (or "tablespace") storage, it's easy to waste space when defining a table. As usual, we can't say there is a single description that applies to all SQL packages, but — again as usual — the basic methods are likely to have much in common, so it's worth looking at a few space-saving techniques.

The most obvious possibility is to use the *VARCHAR* data type (or, as SQL 92 would have it, *CHARACTER VARYING*). *VARCHAR* allows the field length to vary and thus eliminates all trailing spaces. A *VARCHAR* field typically contains a single byte or word at the beginning meaning "number of bytes following," then the bytes themselves (minus the trailing spaces). Sometimes, using *VARCHAR* will have no effect (many DBMSs simply ignore it and store all character fields in a fixed-size format).

Figure 8.3 illustrates the differences between fixed and variable field storage.

Since we need at least one byte to store the size, a field which is unlikely to contain more than one trailing space should not be defined as *VARCHAR* — *FIRST_INITIAL_OF_PERSONAL_NAME VARCHAR(1)*, for instance, is inadvisable. *VARCHAR* is also usually a bad idea if the values are extremely volatile: updates on *VARCHAR* fields cause records to shrink (wasting space that probably won't be reclaimed until the next database reorganization), or cause records to expand (meaning that the entire row has to be moved somewhere else if the expanded record can't fit on the same page anymore). Finally, *VARCHAR* fields might lead to slower accesses if the DBMS puts variable-size fields in a different file from the main one (for instance, an xBASE product might use *memo* files, leaving only a pointer to the *memo* record within the *.DBF* record).

If none of the above situations apply, using *VARCHAR* instead of *CHAR* won't hurt. In fact, you will probably save space using *VARCHAR* instead of *INTEGER* — it would take five bytes to store the number 2,489 in a *VARCHAR* field, and 11 bytes to store it in an *INTEGER* field, for instance. In fact, using *VARCHAR* instead of any other data type will almost always save space when the value to be stored is commonly blank, or *NULL*, or shorter than the defined maximum size of the alternative data type. The downside to such spatial thrift is, of course, the loss of automatic input validation and the potential loss of the ability to do arithmetic.

How does your DBMS store a *NULL* "value" for a one-character *CHAR* column? It could use a special value (ASCII *0*, say) with the implied understanding that "ASCII *0* means *NULL*." But *CHAR* fields are supposed to allow *any* character in the range ASCII *0* to ASCII *255*, so special values are a cheat. (What if you wanted to store a *real* ASCII *0*?)

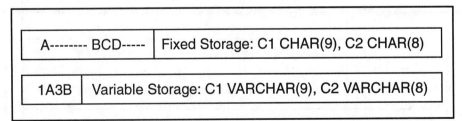

**Figure 8.3**   *Fixed versus variable storage. both records have a defined length of 9 + 8 = 17 bytes, and both contain the same amount (4 bytes) of actual data. The fixed field record uses up all 17 bytes of storage to store "A" in the first column and "BCD" in the second column, but the variable field record uses up only the 4 bytes actually needed to store the data.*

A more robust DBMS will do what IBM's DB2 does — store a one-byte flag at the start of the field, which contains a non-zero value if the field is *NULL*. Figure 8.4 illustrates this technique.

Since the flag byte is needed only if the column can contain *NULL*s, the DBMS won't create the flag byte if you define a column as *NOT NULL*. Thus, if a column is really a *NOT NULL* field and you don't define it as such, you waste one byte per field in every record.

Some database systems, Sybase, for example, treat *NULL* columns as effectively variable in size. When the column is updated, this causes first a deletion of the existing record and then an insertion of the new one. *PC Magazine*[1] found that, because of this, updates are three times faster if a column is defined as *NOT NULL*.

Coding is another technique that saves space, though it usually costs time. For example, suppose a *PROVINCE* column can contain either "Saskatchewan" or "Alberta":

```
CREATE TABLE T
        (PROVINCE CHAR(12))
        CHECK (PROVINCE='Saskatchewan' OR PROVINCE='Alberta');
```

It's obvious that instead of storing the full name of the province, we could store only one byte in this field, such as "*1*" or "*2*" — provided the user (or the application program) knows that, by convention, *1* means Saskatchewan, *2* means Alberta, and nothing else is possible. The trouble is that the SQL engine doesn't know about the convention, so:

```
SELECT PROVINCE FROM T ORDER BY PROVINCE;
```

| \<flag byte\> | \<actual data\> |
|:---:|:---:|
| 0 | ABCDE    -- this field contains *ABCDE* |
| 0 | -- this field contains spaces |
| 1 | -- this field contains NULL |

**Figure 8.4**    *IBM DB2 and its clones store a one-byte flag at the start of the field to indicate the presence of a* NULL *"value."*

would put Saskatchewan before Alberta;

```
SELECT * FROM T WHERE PROVINCE LIKE '%ask%';
```

would return nothing, and so on.

It's better to define the convention as follows:

```
CREATE TABLE LISTOFPROVINCES
        (S1 CHAR(1) NOT NULL PRIMARY KEY, PROVINCE CHAR(12));

INSERT INTO LISTOFPROVINCES VALUES (1,'Saskatchewan');
INSERT INTO LISTOFPROVINCES VALUES (2,'Alberta');

CREATE TABLE T
        (S1 NOT NULL CHAR(1) REFERENCES LISTOFPROVINCES);
```

Table *T* now has a foreign key referencing *LISTOFPROVINCES,* and *LISTOFPROVINCES* contains only the values 1 and 2, so the original *CHECK* clause becomes unnecessary. Now the two problems we originally brought up can be solved by viewing joins or subqueries:

```
SELECT PROVINCE FROM LISTOFPROVINCES, T
        WHERE T.S1 = LISTOFPROVINCES.S1
        ORDER BY PROVINCE;
```

and:

```
SELECT * FROM T WHERE S1 IN
        (SELECT S1 FROM LISTOFPROVINCES
                WHERE PROVINCE LIKE '%ask%');
```

for instance.

But joins are only good for *SELECT* problems, so this is really only a one-way code. For a full coding system that the SQL engine can recognize, we'll have to wait for implementations of the SQL 92 syntax:

```
CASE PROVINCE
        WHEN 1 THEN 'Saskatchewan'
        WHEN 2 THEN 'Alberta'
END
```

When joins occur over a long and non-unique series of indexed columns, you can save space by doing the exact reverse of the above coding technique. Avoid joins entirely by storing all necessary information in one table, even if the information is redundant. This process is known as denormalization. Consider, for instance, tables *A* and *B*, which are designed to join over key *K*. All values of *K* are stored four times, once each in *A* and *B*, and once each in the indexes to *A* and *B*. (If you combined *A* and *B* into one table, you'd only be storing the *K* values twice, once in the column and once in the index. In fact, since indexes are often created only to speed up joins, it's possible that you'd be able to save the index space too.)

## *Physical Reorganization*

In the mathematical set theory that underpins SQL DBMSs, ordering is irrelevant. But in real query situations, users tend to get thrown off by reports that aren't sorted by something. (Look at all the reports your company uses and count the number that are printed in a random order. We predict that the answer is zero.) If a certain table tends to be shown in order by a certain column or group of columns — the primary key, for instance — then there's an advantage to storing the records in that order. The advantage is not so much in the sorting itself (a tournament sort is not aided if all records are already in order), but in the later output. If one doesn't have to jump around in the file much, there will be less disk I/O. The fact will not be noticeable with a small number of records because they'll all be in a cache anyway, but that doesn't change the point.

The trouble is, records in a database won't "just happen" to be in order by the desired values. A normal DBMS will insert new data at the end of the file, in which case the ordering is by the date of entry — often not the perfect choice for an output sequence.

If the DBMS stores *VARCHAR* columns as a truly variable-size field, there's an additional problem: what does it do when the current size of an existing record at the start of the file is three characters and now the user updates it so that the size becomes four characters? It won't fit anymore, so the DBMS has to delete it and put it at the end of the file.

The reclamation of space for deleted records is generally not automatic. Don't bet that the statement:

```
DELETE FROM T WHERE S1=0;
```

will reduce the size of the file containing table *T*'s rows. In the mainframe world, someone comes during the night and cleans up after the day's inserts and updates and deletes. However, microcomputer operating systems lack the equivalent *TOOTHFAIRY.EXE* component. It is important to reorganize from time to time then, if your files are getting big and change a lot.

Of course, every vendor will supply some sort of *ORGANIZE.EXE* utility program for the job, but if you want to maintain your databases using standard SQL and/or ODBC, you're better off avoiding vendor-specific utilities when you can write your own. Usually the following reorganization plan will work:

For each table in the database:

a) save all the information about the table that you will need to re-create it

b) *SELECT * FROM <table> ORDER BY <primary key>;* exporting results to a file

c) *DROP TABLESPACE;* or the equivalent

d) *CREATE TABLE* again, based on the information you saved

e) *INSERT INTO <table>;* importing the file contents saved in step (b)

If you use a database package that supports clustering, then this reorganization should be unnecessary. Though automatic clustering of data (in order by, say, a primary key) is an important topic, we avoid discussing it because implementations differ so radically among vendors who support it.[2] Anyway, the initial load of a clustered table is usually helped along by pre-sorting the input data.

# Indexes

Back in Chapter 6, we discussed indexes and mentioned in passing that indexes are also used to "ensure that *UNIQUE, PRIMARY KEY*, and *FOREIGN KEY* constraints are maintained." We now return to that topic.

# Uniqueness

Here is a common test for ANSI SQL compliance, failed by even the good packages:

```
/* If your DBMS won't do this, it doesn't follow ANSI SQL rules */
CREATE TABLE T (S1 INT NOT NULL);
/* or CREATE TABLE T (S1 INT NOT NULL, UNIQUE(S1)); */
CREATE UNIQUE INDEX I ON T (S1);
INSERT INTO T VALUES (1);
INSERT INTO T VALUES (2);
UPDATE T SET S1=S1+1;
```

In other words: before the update takes place, table *T* has two unique values:

| S1 |
| --- |
| 1 |
| 2 |

After the update, table *T* will *still* have two unique values:

| S1 |
| --- |
| 2 |
| 3 |

If the update is done on the set of *T's* values (the way the ANSI SQL standard specifies it should) there is no problem. In reality, though, the SQL engine normally does the update one row at a time, so first it changes the first value found from *1* to *2*. Then it changes the second value found from *2* to *3*.

That means there's an intermediate point where the index would have two non-unique values:

| S1 |
| --- |
| 2 |
| 2 |

So, if your DBMS rejects the update (with an error return saying "*UNIQUE* constraint violated") that's because it's testing for uniqueness at the time it changes the row — which is far more efficient, because at that time it just happens to have the correct page of the index in front of it.

Would you rather have a package that, instead of ignoring the standard in order to do updates quickly, waits till all updates are done, then does a completely separate pass through the index file to check for violations? No you wouldn't, thinks your DBMS vendor, who's probably right.

## *Primary and Foreign Keys*

If you create a table with a *PRIMARY KEY*, you're likely to need an index because primary keys must be unique and, as we've seen, uniqueness is best supported by creating a unique index.

If you create a table with a *FOREIGN KEY*, you're likely to need an index too, because when you update or delete the primary key that this foreign key references, you have to look up the old foreign key value to make sure it's not there anymore.

It is therefore not improbable that your DBMS will create a [unique] index automatically whenever you create a table with a referential-integrity constraint. To find out whether your DBMS does this, you can use the "checking for indexes" routine in Chapter 6.

## *Data Imports*

On a data import, should you *CREATE INDEX* before or after importing the data?

| Case I: | or | Case II: |
|---|---|---|
| CREATE TABLE | | CREATE TABLE |
| CREATE UNIQUE INDEX | | <<10000 INSERTs>> |
| <<10000 INSERTs>> | | CREATE UNIQUE INDEX |

The database package vendor probably has a special optimized routine designed to handle Case II because creating an index on an already-existing data set is one of the most popular benchmarks used in computer magazine reviews. The obvious optimization is to do a "tournament sort" of the keys; notice that when we add keys to an index one at a time we are in effect performing an "insertion sort" or "bridge sort," which is wildly inferior (read your Knuth).

But would you choose Case II even if you knew there was a slight chance the keys were not unique (which means that the database would not be "valid" after the inserts)? Yes, you would, we think. Database users will often choose Case II anyway in order to save time. This leads to a tip: If there's a large amount of data that you're about to update, say changing more than 50 percent of the keys in the table, first drop the indexes on that table, then do the update, then create the indexes again:

```
big_update ()
{
exec sql drop index i;
exec sql update t set s1 = s1 + s2;
exec sql create index i on t (s1);
if (error -- non-unique) {
    exec sql rollback; }
else {
    execsql commit; }
}
```

Even more extremely, instead of:

```
DELETE FROM T;
```

you might find this faster:

```
DROP TABLE T;
CREATE TABLE T (S1 ...,S2);
```

That is, drop the table entirely and then recreate it so that an empty table *T* exists.

Warning: These tricks get somewhat trickier if your DBMS cannot roll back a *DROP* statement (see the section on *COMMIT/ROLLBACK* later in this chapter).

The moral is: Vendors will violate the ANSI SQL standard, and users will temporarily violate relational integrity, if it speeds up indexing.

## *Saving Space in Index Files*

Index files (or "indexspaces") differ from data files in an obvious and critical respect: the keys are in order. The best techniques simply take advantage of this fact. The DBMS vendor who knows about these techniques can reduce the space required for index files dramatically.

The techniques we'll talk about are front-truncation, back-truncation, automatic balancing, interspersed index keys, bit lists, and radix-40 storage.

## *Front-truncation*

Front-truncation of index keys should be a feature in all but the most primitive database packages.

For example, suppose we have a table called *MEMBERS_OF_PARLIAMENT*, based on Canadian members of Parliament, with an index based on their surnames:

| Key Value | Size |
|-------------|------|
| CHAREST | 7 |
| CHRÉTIEN | 8 |
| CHRISTOPHER | 11 |
| CLARK | 5 |
| CLARKE | 6 |
| total | 37 |

Since the index keys are in order, there will tend to be lots of duplication at the front of each key — all the keys that begin with *CH* are together, for instance. A DBMS vendor can take advantage of that duplication with this conventional rule of front-truncation: "The first byte of an index key contains the number of bytes in the rest of the key that duplicate the bytes in the same ordinal positions of the previous key."

A front-truncated index on *MEMBERS_OF_PARLIAMENT* would look like this:

| Key Value | Size |
|-----------|------|
| [0]CHAREST | 8 |
| [2]RÉTIEN | 7 |
| [3]ISTOPHER | 9 |
| [1]LARK | 5 |
| [5]E | 2 |
| total | 31 |

The space saving in this case is six bytes, or 16%. Since the chance of duplication in the first bytes increases with the number of keys in the index, the saving would be a considerably greater percentage in a large index. Front-truncation costs practically nothing, so if the DBMS supports it, it's usually automatic and not optional.

Here's a dilemma, then. Suppose *MEMBERS_OF_PARLIAMENT* actually has two columns, *PARTY* and *SURNAME*. The *PARTY* column has only two possible values. The *SURNAME* column has 300 possible values. What's the best way to make a compound index based on these two columns? There are two possibilities.

The first possibility:

```
CREATE INDEX I ON MEMBERS_OF_PARLIAMENT(PARTY,SURNAME);
```

creates the following index:

| Key Value | Size | Front-Truncated Value | Size |
|-----------|------|-----------------------|------|
| CONSERVATIVE,CHAREST | 20 | [0]CONSERVATIVE,CHAREST | 21 |
| CONSERVATIVE,CLARK | 18 | [14]LARK | 5 |
| CONSERVATIVE,CLARKE | 19 | [18]E | 2 |
| LIBERAL,CHRÉTIEN | 16 | [0]LIBERAL,CHRÉTIEN | 17 |
| LIBERAL,CHRISTOPHER | 19 | [11]ISTOPHER | 9 |
| total | 92 | total | 54 |

The second possibility:

```
CREATE INDEX I ON MEMBERS_OF_PARLIAMENT(SURNAME,PARTY);
```

creates the following index:

| Key Value | Size | Front-Truncated Value | Size |
|-----------|------|-----------------------|------|
| CHAREST,CONSERVATIVE | 20 | [0]CHAREST,CONSERVATIVE | 21 |
| CHRÉTIEN,LIBERAL | 16 | [2]RÉTIEN,LIBERAL | 15 |
| CHRISTOPHER,LIBERAL | 19 | [3]ISTOPHER,LIBERAL | 17 |
| CLARK,CONSERVATIVE | 18 | [1]LARK,CONSERVATIVE | 18 |
| CLARKE,CONSERVATIVE | 19 | [5]E,CONSERVATIVE | 15 |
| total | 92 | total | 86 |

If the compound index key order is *(PARTY, SURNAME)* rather than *(SURNAME, PARTY)*, then the size of the index is 35 percent smaller. So, if we're only concerned with saving space, then that's the order we should choose for our index keys. However, while a *(PARTY, SURNAME)* compound index is best for searches that use expressions like: *WHERE PARTY=...* or *WHERE PARTY=... AND SURNAME=...*, it doesn't do very well on searches that ask only: *WHERE SURNAME=....* Such searches are served poorly by an index that doesn't start with *SURNAME*; in fact some DBMSs won't bother to use index *I* if the first field in the index key doesn't match the first field in the *WHERE* clause.

So the answer to our question — "How do you make a compound index?" — should be "What am I going to use the compound index for?"

You can use the DBMS on this book's diskette to test the effects of front- and back- truncation. A sample exercise is in the commented file *SAMPLE1.C*. You can also do a simple test on your own DBMS: If you have a separate index file and it doubles in size every time you double the number of keys, you know it's not using either front- or back- truncation — a clue that the index routines are unsophisticated.

## Back-truncation

The last example had a lot of redundancy towards the end of the index key. Suppose we decide that we want a compound index on *(SURNAME, PARTY)*, because most of our searches are going to be of the *WHERE SURNAME=*... variety but a few will be *WHERE SURNAME=... AND PARTY=*....

Back-truncation compresses indexes more drastically than front-truncation. The rule is: "Throw out any trailing bytes in the index key which do not help distinguish this key from the previous or next keys."

Using back-truncation and *(SURNAME, PARTY)* as the compound index key, we'd end up with the following index:

| Key Value | Size | Back-Truncated Value | Size |
|-----------|------|----------------------|------|
| CHAREST,CONSERVATIVE | 20 | CHA | 3 |
| CHRÉTIEN,LIBERAL | 16 | CHRÉ | 4 |
| CHRISTOPHER,LIBERAL | 19 | CHRI | 4 |
| CLARK,CONSERVATIVE | 18 | CLARK, | 6 |
| CLARKE,CONSERVATIVE | 19 | CLARKE | 6 |
| total | 92 | total | 23 |

Notice the information loss. You can't tell from the index what party *CHRISTOPHER* belongs to. In fact, you can't even be sure the third key *is* *CHRISTOPHER*.

But here's what you *can* tell from the index: the search *WHERE SURNAME='CHRISTOPHER' AND PARTY='LIBERAL'* won't be satisfied by the *CHA*, *CHRÉ*, *CLARK*, or *CLARKE* keys — the *only* candidate that satisfies the requirements is *CHRI*. (Remember, the rule said we have to leave enough in the keys so that the DBMS can distinguish between them.) All the SQL engine has to do is read the actual record that the *CHRI* key points to, and check if the predicate is true or false. That's only one extra disk access.

Our final list illustrates the effect of combining front- and back-truncation:

| Key Value | Size | Truncated Value | Size |
|---|---|---|---|
| CHAREST,CONSERVATIVE | 20 | [0]CHA | 4 |
| CHRÉTIEN,LIBERAL | 16 | [2]RÉ | 3 |
| CHRISTOPHER,LIBERAL | 19 | [2]I | 2 |
| CLARK,CONSERVATIVE | 18 | [1]LARK | 5 |
| CLARKE,CONSERVATIVE | 19 | [5]E | 2 |
| total | 92 | total | 16 |

Our space saving now is about 83 percent. But we pay for this with an extra disk access on every search (and several extra disk accesses on updates). Disk space is cheap at the moment, so back-truncation isn't a popular option.

## Automatic Balancing

Automatic balancing isn't exactly a compression technique, but it fits in our discussion of saving index space. To test if you've got it, simply delete all the rows in a large indexed table. If the index file remains the same size, that means your DBMS is not reclaiming space taken by deleted keys.

Now take a large table, *T*, with an index on an integer column, *C*, and:

```
UPDATE T SET C = C - 10000;
```

If the index file increases in size, that means your DBMS isn't ensuring that all index pages have the same number of keys — an effect called "unbalancing," which, as well as wasting space, can have a bad impact on performance. In that case, your DBMS vendor should have provided a separate utility program for index maintenance.

## Interspersed Index Keys

Interspersed index keys can save both space and time. If your DBMS allows you to specify that two different indexes can be stored in the same index file, you may have this feature. However, there's two possible ways to do it; interspersing the keys and not interspersing the keys.

To exemplify, we'll split our *MEMBERS_OF_PARLIAMENT* table into two separate tables, *LIBERALS* and *CONSERVATIVES*, and make two separate indexes, specifying that the indexes should be in the same index file. Our result will be one of these two possibilities:

| Non-interspersed index |
|---|
| [index page #1: CONSERVATIVES only] |
| CHAREST |
| CLARK |
| CLARKE |
| [index page #2: LIBERALS only] |
| CHRÉTIEN |
| CHRISTOPHER |

| Interspersed index |
|---|
| [index page #1: "either"] |
| CHAREST [CONSERVATIVE] |
| CHRÉTIEN [LIBERAL] |
| CHRISTOPHER [LIBERAL] |
| CLARK [CONSERVATIVE] |
| CLARKE [CONSERVATIVE] |

The non-interspersed index seems to be the case used with dBASE IV .MDX index files, and is of no interest in this discussion.

The interspersed index file has the keys for different tables mixed together. The primary sort order is by the key itself, not the index type. Interspersing improves the chances for front-truncation, but the real theoretical advantage in the SQL world is for equi-joins. If two rows are from two different tables but have the same index-key values, and those keys are interspersed in the same file, then those index keys will be together in the same page in the index file. This should mean that the query:

```
SELECT * FROM LIBERALS L, CONSERVATIVES C
     WHERE L.SURNAME='CHRISTOPHER'
     AND L.SURNAME=C.SURNAME;
```

will only need to look at one index leaf page, since all *LIBERAL* and all *CONSERVATIVE CHRISTOPHER*s are likely to be together on that page (especially if the keys are unique).

By the way, you may have noticed that our example list has *CHRÉTIEN* before *CHRISTOPHER* because we expect that's where literate people would look for it. Test your DBMS: does it reverse the order because the letter É follows the letter I in the MS-DOS and Windows character sets? It's not a failure if it does, because SQL 92 covers this matter of collating sequences quite confusingly — but you can forget about using it to keep track of the Parliament of Canada. (And if you think collating letters with accent marks really isn't relevant to English, check what order your Webster's Dictionary puts these words in: charge/chargé; lame/lamé; pate/paté; pique/piqué; resume/résumé.)

## *Bit Lists*

Bit lists are perhaps the ultimate in condensation, taking only one bit per record. For example, if we have eight records in our database, and they contain a field whose only possible values are *MALE* and *FEMALE*, we can store the data in an 8-bit bit list:

*/ 0 / 1 / 0 / 0 / 0 / 0 / 0 / 0*

In this example, the second record is *FEMALE (1)* and the rest are *MALE*.

A bit list is not a true index because it does not contain a pointer field: the record address is derived from the bit's relative position in the list. Searching a bit list is fast (you can test 32 records at a time with a single assembler *CMPSD* instruction). This is the secret of FoxPro's "Rushmore" technology, but in an SQL context truly binary values are rare. In a real world situation, the possible values of a bit in the bit-list for *SEX* would have to allow for *MALE, FEMALE, NULL*, and *<record deleted>* — FoxPro, like all dBASE clones, ignores the last two possibilities, so searches can deliver inapplicable or deleted records.

## *Radix-40 Storage*

Radix-40 storage is the final space-saving option we'll mention. The idea is arithmetically simple: there are 2 to the 16th power, or 65,536 possible bit combinations in a 16-bit word. Allowing for 26 letters in the alphabet, plus 10 digits, plus apostrophe, dash, comma, and space, we have a character set with 40 possible values. But 40 cubed (40*40*40) is only 64,000. In other words, there are only 64,000 possible three-character combinations in this 40-value character set.

Therefore, three characters can fit in one 16-bit word instead of just two if we use an appropriate encoding scheme. If your DBMS doesn't do case-sensitive searches and ignores most special or control characters, it might be using radix-40 index storage.

# *Page Sizes*

Operating systems transfer data to and from the disk in a fixed size unit which we'll call a transfer unit. (Every operating system seems to have a different name for it — a block, a sector, a cluster — but these terms can also have other meanings.) Your application will run more efficiently if the page size of your DBMS is equal to (or some factor of) the transfer unit of the operating system.

Index files have fixed page sizes, usually some multiple of 512 bytes. With some DBMS packages, the data files are also in fixed pages — or, if the file format is fixed-field, one can manipulate the table definition so that there will effectively be no splitting of data over, say, a 512-byte boundary. If the page size is manipulable, there's usually no easy rule for how to do it, and the manual for your DBMS probably gives no good advice, because the effect of changing page size is dependent on the disk drive, the operating system, and the utilities you happen to be using.

You can determine the transfer unit of the operating system by checking the "cluster size" (or "block size," etc.) and the "number of sectors per cluster" for a given hard drive; the assembler routine for finding this information is available in most hardware introductory texts for IBM PC-compatible machines.

But if you're using a caching disk interface like Microsoft's SMARTDRV, remember that it tries to read and write to disk a track at a time, usually eight or nine sectors at once. If you're using a network, remember that the adapter card probably deals in buffers which have a fixed size, usually a multiple of 512. And, finally, if you're using a disk compression routine based on the Lempel-Ziv algorithm, remember that this scheme counts the relative frequency of bytes in a given area, usually 8Kb, so the disk compression reads and writes in 8Kb blocks.

Because of the many factors involved, you'll probably have to fine-tune the page size by trial and error — run a benchmark with a small or uneven page size, reorganize the table, and run the benchmark again. If even that's too tough, just try to ensure that you're using 512- or 2048- or 4096- or 8192-byte page sizes (if you must use .*DBF* files, the header will be a problem because it won't have the same size as the data records, but this is not insuperable).

# The Importance of a Good Sort Algorithm

Obviously a DBMS calls a sorting routine when its SQL engine gets a *SELECT* statement with an *ORDER BY* clause. Less obviously, the DBMS can call a sort routine when it has to check for duplicate values because in order to check for a duplication of value[x] in a sorted set, it only has to compare value[x] with value[x-1] and value[x+1], rather than with all values between value[0] and value[max].

Therefore, *SELECT DISTINCT*, *COUNT(DISTINCT COLUMN)*, and *UNION SELECT ...* usually involve a call to a sort routine.

*GROUP BY* also requires a check for duplicate values — the only difference is that *GROUP BY* keeps duplicates and *DISTINCT* gets rid of them — so *SELECT ... GROUP BY ...* also implies a call to a sort routine.

Merging two ordered lists is faster than merging two unordered lists, so a join on two unindexed columns goes better if they are sorted in advance. Again, the DBMS has to call a sort routine.

Finally, adding one key at a time to an index (which could in effect be a "bridge sort") is more efficient if one starts with a set of keys which have been pre-ordered using a better algorithm than a bridge sort — which means *CREATE INDEX* probably involves a call to a sort routine.

Since these operations are frequently encountered, it's a good idea to consider what the sort routine does. The best algorithm in common use today is the "tournament sort" described by Knuth in 1966.

This algorithm has these features: the number of comparisons goes up logarithmically as the number of rows to be sorted goes up linearly, with the ideal formula dependent on the $\log_2$ of the number of items; it doesn't help much if the rows are already in order; and the speed gets dramatically better if tags are cached or permanently stored in RAM — in other words, make sure there's lots of room before asking the DBMS to do a big sort.

Because sorts of large sets can use large amounts of RAM (generally larger than a 64Kb segment), and because the most time is spent on comparisons (which will go twice as fast if one can do four bytes at a time rather than two bytes at a time), a timid prediction is possible. It is in sort routines that we can expect the most dramatic gains — probably at least a factor of 2 — as the changeover from 16-bit to 32-bit operating systems and compilers gathers momentum.

We can't leave this subject without mentioning, rather plaintively, that "sorting" means "putting things in order."

## *Commit/Rollback*

When dBASE IV was in gestation, one columnist thusly described a surprising new feature:

"... I use this new *SET* command in a demonstration at my seminars, and it always causes an uproar. I start *BROWSE* in dBASE IV and begin changing a field in several records to a new value. After five or six records are changed, I suddenly turn off the computer. When the computer is restarted, and the severe dBphobics are helped back into their chairs, I open the data file again in *BROWSE* and the changes I had made before turning off the power are still there. This is definitely worth waiting for ...."[3]

We quote this article as a joke. "So dBASE III was supposed to be a database system, was it?," we cluck. "Well, *real* database systems have always had a method to guarantee that data will be saved." To quote ANSI SQL 86:

"<Commit statement> ... Any changes to the database that were made by the current transaction are committed."[4]

Now ask yourself soberly: does your database package really support *COMMIT* and *ROLLBACK*? Will it always pass this test? There are a couple of reasons why you should be unsure.

Foremost and first, look at your *CONFIG.SYS* and *AUTOEXEC.BAT* files and check what sort of a cache program you're using (of course you're using one, and of course it's been running so smoothly that you nearly forgot it's there). If it's Microsoft's *SMARTDRV.SYS*, the *CONFIG.SYS* line probably looks like this:

```
device=c:\win\smartdrv.sys 2048 256 /a
```

This is dangerous. *SMARTDRV.SYS*'s default action (at least with MS-DOS v6.0) is to cache writes. Effectively, then, *SMARTDRV* "lies" to your DBMS at *COMMIT* time: when the SQL engine says "write to the disk," *SMARTDRV* intercepts the operating system command and returns "write complete" *entire seconds before it actually attempts to do the write*. The

SQL engine then innocently passes the lie on to the host program: it returns *sqlcode=0* "OK."

To see how this works, try inserting 10,000 rows into a table which has many indexes, then *COMMIT* and pull the plug immediately as soon as the host program gets the "OK" message back. Then plug back in and check whether the database's indexes are corrupt. Don't forget to run *CHKDSK* too. (Er ... by the way, you might just want to do this as a "thought experiment" if you have serious jobs to do.)

You can fix *SMARTDRV* by changing the default settings in the *CONFIG.SYS* file, but you'll have more trouble turning off Novell NetWare's write caching (Novell's speed seems to depend on this "feature"), and for most caching programs you won't have any idea what they're up to at all. (Do you know anything about OS/2's, say?)

So, although your ANSI handbook and your DBMS manual might suggest that *COMMIT* guarantees that the data is really on disk and is recoverable, forget it: there are no guarantees if you have a cache.

End of warning. Now, how does an SQL package actually support *COMMIT* and *ROLLBACK* for changes to the database? Consider this instruction sequence:

```
INSERT INTO T (COLUMN1) VALUES (1);
COMMIT;
```

## Method 1: Logging

At *INSERT* time, the DBMS will write to a log file, that a *1* has been inserted at the end of the data file. If the DBMS is any good, it closes the log file after the write and then re-opens it — this helps ensure that the file directory is updated for a file that's growing. After this, it actually does the *INSERT* and updates the indexes (probably using in-RAM buffers), then it writes the buffers to disk. Finally, at *COMMIT* time, the DBMS writes to the log again — just a message this time saying "commit happened here."

So: if the power goes off sometime during the *INSERT* or anytime before the *COMMIT*, the DBMS can recover when it starts up again — it looks at the end of the log file and sees that the "commit happened here" is missing from the last log entry, so it looks at the end of the file and deletes the inserted row if it's there, then looks in all indexes for table *T* and deletes any keys that got inserted for the row that didn't really make it in.

Effectively, then, the DBMS does a *ROLLBACK* by reversing any items at the end of the log file that aren't marked as committed.

The logging method is about as safe as reasonably possible given the nature of the operating environment, and delivers the additional advantage of a log file that can be used for audit and backup purposes. The problem is that every transaction requires at least two extra disk accesses to maintain the log file.

## *Method 2: Delayed Writing*

Unlike logging, where the DBMS writes to the database but can reverse the write if *COMMIT* doesn't happen, with the "delayed writing" method the DBMS simply never writes to the database before *COMMIT* time at all. Copies of changed or new pages are simply kept in RAM (if the RAM overflows, then a temporary file is created). At *COMMIT* time, the DBMS will write all changed pages to the database files, then close and re-open all database files so that the file directories will be updated immediately.

So: if the power goes off sometime during the *INSERT* or anytime before the *COMMIT*, the DBMS doesn't need to recover when it starts up again: nothing was written to the database itself.

Delayed writing is much faster than logging provided that the transactions are short so that all changed pages can be kept in RAM without requiring a temporary file. The danger with delayed writing is that a precisely timed physical failure at *COMMIT* time, occurring after some, but not all changed pages have been written to the disk, results in a database with inconsistencies.

Either way — with delayed writing or with logging — it's a good idea to *COMMIT* frequently and thus reduce the amount of data that's being held in temporary logs or unwritten files.

## *Method 3: Cowardly Avoidance*

Some microcomputer-based SQL packages have automatic *COMMIT* as an "option." When instructions are entered online, it is normal (and appropriate) to have automatic *COMMIT* on — but not within transactions. However, sometimes you'll find that *COMMIT* happens to be the default and is recommended in the manual, and sometimes you'll find that only *UPDATE*, *INSERT*, and *DELETE* can be rolled back: all database-definition commands such as *CREATE*, *GRANT*, or *DROP* are subject to automatic *COMMIT*.

The fact is: "automatic commit option" means "no transaction control." If you find that for one reason or another you usually have to operate with the option on, it's appropriate to wonder whether the package you're using really supports `COMMIT` and `ROLLBACK` as something that it expects programmers to use, or whether these commands were just thrown in so that somebody could put a check mark against a box on one of those forms that database vendors are constantly receiving:

```
COMMIT/ROLLBACK supported? (circle one) YES NO
```

To conclude: with the microcomputer operating systems we're using today, your DBMS can't entirely guarantee security. Often the DBMS doesn't try very hard anyway because `COMMIT`s and `ROLLBACK`s slow the benchmarks down. In general, though, we really are better off than in the days of dBASE IV's introduction.

## *Catalog Maintenance*

The database catalog is an ordinary-looking set of database tables defined by the DBMS vendor which contain information about tables defined by the user. In other words, the tables in the database catalog are meta-tables (tables that describe tables). Any change in the *definition* of a user table (a DDL command, e.g., `CREATE TABLE`, `DROP TABLE`, etc.) causes a *manipulation* of the catalog tables which could theoretically be expressed as a series of DML `UPDATE`, `INSERT`, and `DELETE` commands. Or at least that's the way it appears when you have an SQL implementation that allows you to query the catalog and find out information about the database tables with useful statements like:

```
SELECT SUM(LENGTH) FROM SYSCOLUMNS;
```

or:

```
SELECT NAME,TEXT FROM SYSVIEWS;
```

So why can't we operate on these meta-tables just as we operate on regular database tables? Here are examples of some DDL commands and the theoretical DML catalog operations that would have the same result:

| DDL Commands (entered by user) | DML Commands (equivalent operation on catalog) |
|---|---|
| CREATE TABLE T<br>(S1 SMALLINT) | INSERT INTO SYSTABLES ...<br>INSERT INTO SYSCOLUMNS ... |
| ALTER TABLE T<br>ADD S2 CHAR(5) | INSERT INTO SYSCOLUMNS<br>(NAME,TBNAME,COLTYPE,COLLENGTH)<br>VALUES ('S2','T','CHAR',5) |
| ALTER TABLE T<br>MODIFY S1 INTEGER | UPDATE SYSCOLUMNS<br>SET COLTYPE='INTEGER'<br>WHERE NAME='S1'<br>AND TBNAME='T' |
| DROP TABLE T | DELETE FROM SYSCOLUMNS WHERE<br>TBNAME='T'<br>DELETE FROM SYSTABLES WHERE<br>NAME='T' |
| GRANT ALL<br>ON T TO PETER | INSERT INTO SYSTABAUTH ... |
| REVOKE ALL ON<br>T FROM PETER | DELETE FROM<br>SYSTABAUTH ... |
| COMMENT<br>ON TABLE T<br>IS 'HELLO' | UPDATE SYSTABLES SET<br>COMMENT<br>='HELLO' WHERE NAME='T' |

But in fact no SQL implementation offers the simplification of replacing DDL commands with equivalent DML operations on the catalog. The excuse is, "It's dangerous to fool with the catalog," but we suspect something else: it's because catalog tables aren't stored in the same form as ordinary tables. If they were, you'd see that a DBMS package's specs had the same number for "number of tables definable in database" and "maximum number of rows in a table" (since each table created takes up one row in *SYSTABLES*), which is rarely the case. In fact, the whole package is probably customized with special routines to handle the maintenance of the catalog in a specific form — a customization that can be performed for catalog tables because the vendor knows in advance what the table structure is, which isn't the case for user-defined tables.

Incidentally, this might explain the fact that some SQL packages automatically and non-optionally *COMMIT* after every DDL instruction. Dropped something? Want to roll it back? Forget it, it's gone. A far cry from ANSI, but understandable if you consider that the catalog tables aren't really tables in the ordinary sense, so the routines that support transactions on ordinary tables, including the *COMMIT/ROLLBACK* routines that we described earlier, wouldn't be applicable.

With ODBC, even selecting from catalog tables is unsanctioned. You're expected to use various library-function calls to find information in the catalog. This is a shame, because no set of function calls is as rich in power as an SQL *SELECT* statement: the *SELECT* is built for the purpose, and it's a piece of syntax that everyone working with SQL programming knows anyway.

With some trepidation, then, we will continue to use *SELECT*s on the database catalog. ODBC won't actually attempt to stop us because, after all, the syntax of the *SELECT* statements is valid. Yes, we'll have a devil of a time writing portable code this way. But (as the "Is it indexed?" example program shown in Chapter 6 illustrates) it's not impossible yet.

Note that this section was written without reference to the ways that one can access "meta-data" using Microsoft Access. We understand that some of the things which we say "are never done" are, in fact, being pioneered by that product.

## *Comparing a dBASE Update with an SQL Update*

Suppose there is a database with a table named *T* and a field named *F*. The fifteenth record in this table has a value for *F* equal to *0*. There is a user named *Trudy*. She suddenly decides to change the record so that *F = 1*.

With dBASE, which is somewhat of a straw man in this exposition, the affair is straightforward:

1) Open the file named *T*.

2) Read the file header and the field headers so that the size of a record, the position of field *F* within a given record, and the position of the first record in the file (i.e., just after the header) are known.

3) Multiply the record size by 15 (because it's the fifteenth record), add the position of field *F*, and add the start of the first record.

4) Seek to that location in the file.

5) Write *1* in the location you just seeked to.

There is really nothing else to consider. There is a one-to-one correspondence between tables and files; index changes are not automatic so an *UPDATE TABLE* instruction doesn't imply "update indexes too." Records and fields are fixed size and defined clearly in the headers. There are no security checks or integrity checks or validation tests because such concepts are unknown. The file need not be closed.

Now let's see what the same operation requires with a simple single-user SQL package. (The application and the DBMS are on the same computer.)

1) Authorization test: open the catalog file. Find the user record for *Trudy*. If she has system-administration privileges she can do the update. Else find the record for table *T*. If the creator's name = '*TRUDY*,' she can do the update. Else find all grant records where *(grantee = 'TRUDY' or grantee = 'PUBLIC') and TABLE = 'T' and (grant type = 'UPDATE' or grant type = 'ALL') and (grant* is on whole table or *grant* is specifically for *field = 'F'*). If any such records exist, then she can do the update. If all these tests fail, the update is disallowed.

2) Validity test: field *F* is numeric, and *1* is a number, so we pass the most basic test: domains.

3) Integrity test #1: check the catalog entry for table *T*. If field *F* is a unique key (or a component of a unique key), then there will be an index on the key. Look up the value *1* in that index. If it exists, then the update violates the uniqueness constraint, so the update is disallowed.

4) Integrity test #2: check the catalog entry for table *T*. If field *F* is a primary key (or a component of a primary key), then there will be an index on the key. Look up the value *1* in that index. If it exists, then the update violates the uniqueness constraint, so the update is disallowed.

5) Integrity test #3: check the catalog entry for table *T*. If field *F* is a primary key (or a component of a primary key), then for all foreign keys which reference this table with *RESTRICT* — that is, for every table with *CREATE TABLE x ... FOREIGN KEY ... REFERENCES T ON UPDATE RESTRICT*, there will be an index on the foreign key. Look up the value *0* in that index. If it exists, then there is a foreign key referencing primary key *F* that is equal to *0*, so the update is disallowed.

6) Find the record with a serial value of 15 by looking it up in an index or something. (We leave the details vague. Calculating the physical address is very unlikely to be a simple arithmetic calculation as it is with dBASE, although some SQL packages do support ROWID as an option.)

7) Read the entire record into a RAM buffer. Make a copy of the RAM buffer (we'll need to know the original value of *F* when we change index keys, and we'll need to know the values of other fields if they're referenced in *CHECK* clauses or multiple-column indexes, see below). Change the RAM buffer so that *F=1*. *Do not rewrite to disk yet.*

8) *CHECK* clause test: search the catalog for any *CHECK* records for table *T*; for instance, if the table creation was done with *CREATE TABLE T ... CHECK (F>G)*, the DBMS would now have to check whether, in the record it's currently looking at, the new value of *F*, i.e., *1*, is greater than the current value in field *G*.

9) By looking in the catalog, find all indexes on table *T* which contain field *F*. Notice that, unlike dBASE, SQL indexes can have multiple columns. For instance, an index could be made with *CREATE UNIQUE INDEX I ON T (G,F)* — so look up key value = *'..','0'* in index *I* and delete it, then insert key value = *'..','1'*. These changes are still being done to RAM copies of the index pages. Of course, if there are any unique indexes whose uniqueness would be violated because there is already an *F='1'* component in them, then the DBMS would simply throw away all the changed in-RAM copies and return an error code to the host program: "cannot update, unique key duplicated."

10) Open the log file (the rule is: always write to the log first, then do the actual database update second). Seek to the end of the log file, add an entry to the effect that user *Trudy* is doing *UPDATE T SET F='1'* on such-and-such a record, and don't forget to note that the previous value of *F* was *'0'*. (We'll need that information if we *ROLLBACK*.)

11) Encrypt the record contents in some way. This step is optional and many SQL packages don't even have it as an option. Still, it seems silly to go to all the trouble of checking whether *Trudy* has appropriate SQL authorization if all anyone has to do is run a patch program to change the unencrypted, unprotected file. There might also be some recoding at this point; for instance, a DBMS that runs under both Windows and MS-DOS might do *OEMTOANSI* so that the database storage is consistent.

12) Rewrite the changed record. In this particular case, the size has not changed so we don't have to worry about the details of variable-size records that increase in size and have to be moved.

13) Rewrite the index records.

14) If no disk errors were reported during the rewriting, return "OK" to the host program.

15) Later, when *COMMIT* is encountered, open the log, seek to the end of the log file, write a "successful *COMMIT*" entry, and close the log.

So, the question is: which is faster, dBASE clones or SQL packages? We can't settle that question by benchmarking "How fast does an update happen," because the word "update," to the SQL package, implies a far more complex series of steps. In an equestrian Grand Prix, we don't give a prize to the fastest horse if it doesn't jump over all the fences. Before doing a benchmark, then, look at what the SQL package does that the dBASE clone doesn't do and ask yourself, "Should a DBMS do these things?" If you follow the majority and say, "Well, somebody's got to do it," then to do a valid comparison, you'll have to write a dBASE program that simulates the SQL package's steps. So far, nobody's invested the time to do that. And that answers the question, doesn't it?

(Note: Borland's dBASE IV is in fact capable of doing embedded SQL statements, but reportedly this is done by translating to dBASE code internally. Microsoft's dBASE clone, FoxPro, can handle some SQL queries with reportedly very good results — but not updates, as in our example here.)

## *Operating Systems of the Future*

We already have multitasking 32-bit operating systems — OS/2, Windows NT, NEXTSTEP 486, UNIX, and the list goes on — but we use the heading "Operating Systems of the Future" because, in the present, DBMS packages still have to work with MS-DOS and/or Windows. This is just a look at what the more progressive DBMSs will be able to take advantage of, probably starting with the packages that were originally ported down from minicomputers and which, before now, were a tight fit and couldn't really strut their stuff.

A 32-bit address space is good because SQL products tend to be large. One or two still fit comfortably in the 640Kb of conventional MS-DOS memory, but those are SQL 89 products — the so-far unimplemented SQL 92 is far more complicated, so even the small "non-pigs" are going to have to put on an awful lot of weight now.

A large program is also more efficient if all the code is not split into multiple 64Kb segments. Various limitations — for example, 64Kb maximum record sizes — disappear.

The DBMSs that will benefit most are the ones that currently are the worst: the ones that have been ported down from (32-bit) minicomputers. They had a tough time fitting in an MS-DOS "microcomputer" (Oracle, for example, required a DOS extender for its multiple megabytes of code). Now the port job looks easier.

Multitasking is good because many SQL steps can be done synchronously. For instance, consider the steps that were listed for an SQL "update" operation in the previous section. The various tests that are performed at the start (authorization test, validity test, integrity test, *CHECK* clause test) could all be done at the same time because no test is dependent on the results of another test. If there are several indexes for the record, the DBMS could split up into one thread per key. The application program could regain control immediately after the log record is written, since only an operating system failure could cause a failure after that point.

All in all, the future looks pretty bright.

## References

1. *PC Magazine*, October 12, 1993.

2. For a discussion of this point, see "Physisches Datenbank-Tuning durch Record-Placement," *Datenbank Fokus Magazine*, 03/04, 1993.

3. Adam Green, *Databased Advisor*, June, 1988.

4. *ANSI SQL 86 Standard*, page 68.

# *Appendix*

The purpose of this appendix is to provide some information on SQL packages, books, standards organizations, and anything else we think might be of interest to someone who has picked up a book on programming with SQL and C. We don't claim that our lists are definitive, but we hope we have provided enough information to get you started.

## *List of Vendors*

The following vendors offer commercial packages that are intended to provide, at a minimum, an SQL 89 compliant DBMS with a C interface, useable on a normal non-networked computer under MS-DOS or Windows.

As well as names and contact phone numbers, we've included some comments about most of the products. The comments are whatever we or others find interesting about these products — we intend neither denigration nor praise. We definitely do not endorse the claims of all the vendors in this list.

Btrieve Technologies Inc.
Austin, TX;  Phone (800) 287-4383
Product: Netware SQL, inherited when Btrieve was spun off from Novell Inc.

Coromandel Industries, Inc.
Forest Hills, NY;  Phone (718) 793-7963
Product: Integra Visual Database Builder (DB) includes an ODBC-compliant SQL engine.

Empress Software Inc.
Greenbelt, MD;  Phone (301) 220-1919
Product: Empress RDBMS has an ANSI-standard SQL interface with a C language interface option.

FFE Software
El Cerrito, CA;  Phone (510) 232-6800
Product: FirstSQL RDBMS is an implementation of ANSI standard SQL that works with FirstSQL C, an embedded SQL precompiler for C.

Gupta Corporation
Menlo Park, CA;  Phone (415) 321-9500
Product: SQLBase v5.0 is an SQL database server.

Informix Software Inc.
Lenexa, KS;  Phone (913) 599-7100
Product: Informix-ESQL allows programmers to embed SQL statements in C programs to create a bridge to Informix DBMSs.

Machine Independent Software Corp.
Herndon, VA;  Phone (703) 435-0413
Product: CQL includes shrouded C source code.

Microsoft Corporation
Redmond, WA;  Phone (206) 882-8080
Product: Microsoft SQL Server is an RDBMS for PC networks. Microsoft also provides the Microsoft ODBC Desktop Database Drivers package, which handles a variety of file formats (for example, Paradox and Excel).

Ocelot Computer Services Inc.
Edmonton, AB Canada; Phone (403) 421-4187
Product: OCELOT2 - THE SQL! is a royalty-free, ODBC-compliant
SQL engine with a C precompiler that translates embedded SQL statements into ODBC calls.

Oracle Corp.
Redwood Shores, CA; Phone (415) 506-7000
Product: ORACLE7 operates on a wide variety of platforms.

Page Ahead
Bellevue, WA; Phone (206) 441-0430
Product: Page Ahead would primarily be of interest to people who want
to write their own ODBC drivers.

Q+E Software
Raleigh, NC; Phone (919) 859-2220
Product: Q+E Database Library provides access to many different database file formats and can be called from C. ODBC-compliant.

Quadbase Systems Inc.
Sunnyvale, CA; Phone (408) 738-6989
Product: Quadbase-SQL for Windows is a database engine implemented
as a .DLL whose native file format is dBASE. It provides a C language
API and an embedded SQL precompiler.

Quark Research Corp.
Newington, CT; Phone (203) 666-3870
Product: pdq is a 32-bit SQL engine that works with ODBC-compliant
front-ends.

Raima Corp.
Issaqua, WA; Phone (206) 557-0200
Product: Raima Database Server supports ODBC and Raima Object
Manager's C++ interface.

Stellar Industries
Diamond Bar, CA; Phone (909) 861-7885
Product: Quasar SQL for Windows is shareware.

Watcom Systems Inc.
Waterloo, ON Canada;  Phone (519) 886-3700
Product: Watcom SQL lets you distribute their stand-alone DOS single-user runtime SQL engine royalty-free. ODBC extended-level-2 supported by a separate Windows package.

XDB Systems Inc.
Laurel, MD; Phone (301) 317-6800
Product: XDB-SQL emphasizes its IBM DB2 compatibility. Also supports Microsoft's DDE and ODBC protocols.

## *Organizations*

The following are standards and quasi-standards groups involved with SQL. This list was provided to us by a member of the ANSI X3H2 Committee.

American National Standards Institute (ANSI)
X3H2 Database Standards Committee
11 West 42nd Street
New York, NY 10035
Phone (212) 642-4900  Fax (212) 302-1286

Global Engineering Inc.
2805 McGaw Avenue
Irvine, CA 92714
Phone (800) 854-7179  Fax (714) 261-7892

National Institute for Standards & Technology
Technology A-266
Gaithersberg, MD 20899
Phone (301) 975-3251

National Technical Information Service
5285 Port Royal Road
Springfield, VA 22161
Phone (703) 487-4650

Open Systems Foundation
11 Cambridge Center
Cambridge, MA 02142
Phone (617) 621-8763

SQL Access Group (SAG)
#450, 4699 Old Ironside Drive
Santa Clara, CA 95054
Phone (408) 988-3545  Fax (408) 988-6712

Transaction Processing Council
Shanley Public Relations
#600, 777 North First Street
San Jose, CA 95112

X/Open Foundation
c/o Blanc and Otis Public Relations
ATTN: Steven Curry
#425, 100 Spear Street
San Francisco, CA 94105
Phone (415) 546-8080

# Books

Our "suggested reading" list includes only one book. Everything else we have seen is either of the *"Introduction to SQL for Dummies"* genre or is extracted from some vendor's manual.

Author:    C.J.Date

Title:      *A Guide to the SQL Standard* (First edition, 1987)

Publisher:  Addison-Wesley Publishing Company

Comment:  All books by C.J. Date are good buys. In this one he lays down the early SQL syntax laws. No ambiguity, no blather. He did a revision of the book (*A Guide to the SQL Standard*, Third edition, 1993) for SQL 92 in collaboration with Hugh Darwen. The revision, unfortunately, is much harder to follow.

# Magazines

There are a few database-oriented monthly magazines, but none of them really address the SQL microcomputer programmer.

*Databased Advisor* emphasizes dBASE and its clones, but the number of SQL product reviews is slowly increasing.

*DBMS Magazine* is now more SQL- than dBASE-oriented, but its emphasis on "client/server" architecture makes it more of interest to high-end users.

*Database Programming and Design* is strictly for the mainframe aficionado; however, some of the DB2 tips are applicable to all.

*Datenbank Fokus* is a database magazine published in Germany. If you can read German, you'll find that their articles deal with the subject of SQL specifically for microcomputers far more than their American counterparts do.

No computer magazine has ever attempted a comprehensive "comparative review" of all SQL packages. It's the sort of thing that *PC Magazine* used to do, but their last complete DBMS survey was in 1988.

# *Index*